LEARN HOW TO TAKE A PUNCH

Building Your Startup Isn't A Marathon, It's A Prizefight

Brett J. Fox

ISBN-13: 9798637618422
ISBN-10: 1477123456

Cover design by: Zarnab Durrani
Library of Congress Control Number: 2018675309
Printed in the United States of America

To my family. Blossom, Avery, Mom, Russ,
Millette, Dan, Denni, Steve and Kathy.
I love you all. Dad, I miss you.

CONTENTS

ROUND 1: DO YOU HAVE WHAT IT TAKES TO BE A STARTUP CEO?

What Is It Really Like to Be A Startup CEO?

My heart is beating too fast, and it won't slow down.

It's 3 AM, and I can't sleep. Again. I get out of bed, and I walk to my office. I am shivering, even though the temperature in the house is 72 degrees – nerves. I turn on the computer, and I check my email. Dammit! No email from the new investor, like he promised. Why can't these guys do what they say they are going to do? Why?!?

3:30 AM: I head back to bed. At least I didn't wake up my wife. Maybe, now I can get a little sleep before the alarm wakes me.

5 AM: The alarm goes off. I had just fallen asleep, and now it goes off! Okay, get up and go work out downstairs. The exercise will do me good. I am shivering, as I walk downstairs.

6 AM: Finish the workout. Shower, shave, have my protein shake, read the paper and answer some emails.

7 AM: I kiss my wife and daughter goodbye, get in the car and head to work. Even the bad days are good, but I don't know how good this one is going to be...yet. Steve calls. It's always good talking to Steve. We talk about what's going on in his life for a change. It's a good distraction.

7:30 AM: Starbucks. You have to love it – a Starbucks as part of a gas station. You can fill up your gas tank and your internal caffeine tank at the same time. Genius!

7:45 AM: I am in the office. I respond to emails and make some phone calls.

9 AM: I am meeting with a potential investor, who is a legend in the VC industry. He says to us, "I hate high-margin businesses!" That might be the stupidest thing we've ever heard raising money. I just smile and continue with our presentation. There's no hope in hell we're getting his money.

10:30 AM: There is a phone call with another investor. "Brett, we should have a term sheet for you by the end of the day." How many times have I heard that? "Great," I respond.

11 AM: Operations meeting. Dave and Shoba are just killing it. Demand keeps increasing, and we are meeting it.

The feeling of starting something, nurturing it to grow and seeing customers buy your products is indescribable. Watching your team and fellow employees feel empowered to make things happen is a great feeling. I need to secure that funding, so they can be fully rewarded for their great work.

12 PM: I really want to talk to someone inside the company about my fears and concerns. It is very tempting when you are down, but you can't go there. I've got to take a walk, leave the building, or do something.

I can't share my worries with the employees. I decide to go for a walk around our "campus." It's 75 degrees outside and I am still shivering. I wish the shivering would go away. It won't.

1 PM: We are now having a traffic meeting. It involves reviewing with Mary, our PR person, the status of our various advertising and marketing campaigns and our collateral development. The beautiful thing about today's world, unlike the bingo-card world I started my career in, is that you can measure everything – and we do!

Oh, how I love it! Website traffic is rising. Sample requests continue growing at a high rate. Design wins are increasing, and so is revenue. Mary and I eliminate the ads that aren't converting and schedule new ads, collateral, videos and blog posts.

3 PM: The company meeting is about to start. Remember, Brett, you need to say what you don't mean, as well as what you do mean. The team will fill in the blanks, if you don't.

The meeting goes well. I update everyone on the status of the fund-raising, sales and new product introductions. The team, as usual, had great questions.

5 PM: I'm in my office. Someone on the executive staff let me know that a member of his team was worried, because I frowned when he asked a question about how sales were going. "I frowned? I don't remember that."

I was laughing, but it was a sober reminder. Every word, gesture and frown, every time you raise your voice, every time you leave the office early, every time you leave the office late, every time you arrive at the office early, every time you arrive at the office late and everything that you do is analyzed by the employees.

"I'll say something about that next time I speak to the team." Next time.

5:45 PM: I check my email. There it is!

Subject: Term Sheet

"Brett, my Partners and I are pleased to present to you this term sheet...."

Euphoric, I print out the attached term sheet.

I walk out of my office and scream, "YES!" at the top of my lungs. I then jump two feet into the air, vastly outperforming my vertical leap at the draft combine. (Yes, that's a joke.) Not bad for a 40-something year old, I think to myself. I start reading through the term sheet.

Oh, please. Why did you add that term? Why! It is another problem. Why can't anything be straight-forward? Why?!?

How are we going to solve this? I call our lead investor, and we agree on a strategy to solve the problem. It should work, if the new investor is reasonable. That's a big if in VC land. I have to find a way to get this round closed.

You are responsible, as CEO, for the lives and well-being of your employees and their families. It's not about you. It's about them. I have to find a way.

7 PM: I pack up my briefcase and head home. Traffic usually thins out when I leave the office after 7PM, but I check Waze just in case. Good. I can take 880 to 280 to get home tonight.

7:30 PM: I arrive home. My wife, daughter and I have dinner. My wife and I help our daughter with her homework after dinner.

9:15 PM: My daughter just went to bed, so I catch up on email and work that needs to get done.

11 PM: Finally, it is time for bed. I know I will fall asleep quickly. The question is, will I stay asleep?

3 AM: I wake up from my nightmare. We couldn't close funding. My wife is sound asleep next to me. I am shivering, even though it is 72 degrees. I hate the shivering.

God, do I hate it. I get up and go to my office and turn on the computer to check my email.

How Do You Overcome Entrepreneurial Fear?

I t's Tuesday morning at 9:18 AM. My heart rate suddenly raced to what felt like 200 beats per minute.

I couldn't believe what I was hearing. We had just agreed to terms with a new lead investor. We were in the process of closing the funding. And now "Raul," one of our two existing investors, just said to me, "I think we should sell the company!"

That moment. That Tuesday at 9:18 AM was the first time I really felt fear as an entrepreneur.

"What?" I asked. I stood straight up. I had never lost my cool speaking with Raul before. However, now he had pushed the right button.

Raul smiled at me. I still remember that sadistic smile. Raul then repeated himself. "I think we should sell the company."

Raul was calm. I wasn't. I could literally feel my heart rate spike. Bang, bang, bang went my heart at 200 beats per minute.

My heart rate wouldn't slow down. Could my heart

explode out of my chest? I didn't know, but it sure felt like it could. It was a different game now. I was truly scared and afraid. My heart rate still wouldn't slow down.

The one thing you can't do when you're fearful: Panic.

We've all been there. You know when you rush to make a decision based on another decision. We all know the results are very likely a bad decision. Bad decisions are what happen when you panic. The first thing that I needed to do was calm down. The fear might not go away, but maybe I could at least calm down, so I could start thinking rationally.

It takes time for you to recover from a good panic attack.

I spent the rest of the day on the phone talking to various advisors.

I had to talk with Gill, our other investor, because this was going to affect him. I also had to let the other board members know what was going on. However, the fear never went away. I felt like I was carrying a one-thousand-pound boulder around.

I could literally feel the weight of the fear on me. "Maybe the fear will go away over the weekend?" I thought to myself. The fear didn't go away over the weekend.

"Maybe the fear will go away over the next couple

weeks?" I thought to myself, after the weekend was over. The fear didn't go away over the next couple of weeks.

"Maybe the fear will go away over the next month or two?" I thought to myself after a couple of weeks. The fear didn't go away after the next couple of months. In fact, the fear never went away.

There I was carrying this one-thousand-pound boulder around everywhere. So, what did I do?

I learned to Dance with The Fear. Seth Godin said you need to ask yourself, "How do I dance with the fear?" In other words, the fear is there. You need to accept that the fear isn't going anywhere.

You just need to keep doing what you're doing, regardless of the fear.

That's the trick: You can't obsess about the fear, and...

You can't worry about what will happen if things don't work out, and, above all...

You can't panic. Above all you can't panic.

It sounds easy, doesn't it? Just dance with the fear. The problem is, it's not easy to just dance with the fear.

It's unbelievably hard to dance with the fear. Here are some tricks that I've learned that help me dance with the fear:

A. Your mind is going at million miles a second when you are scared.

What's the antidote? Meditation is a great antidote. Meditation didn't work for me initially. In fact, it took me a while before I realized the positive effect that meditation was having.

There are some great free online resources. My favorite is Tara Brach's website. Meditation will not solve all your problems. However, meditation will keep you more in the moment.

B. You should have a morning routine.

My morning routine consists of exercising, meditation, journaling and reading. It takes maybe an hour.

The exercise starts you off on a positive note, because there's nothing like getting the endorphins going first thing in the morning. Meditating helps to give me focus. The journaling (along with visualizing my day) is designed for me to realize the positive things that are happening.

Finally, I read an inspirational book or story for about five minutes. Since you have a morning routine, it goes to figure...

C. You need an evening routine too.

An evening routine primes you for the next day. When you're really stressed and fearful, your evening routine can remind you of all the things that went well.

My evening routine includes more positive journaling. I write down three things that went well during the day. Even a really bad day has three things that likely went well.

I write down three acts of service I did for others. This could be as simple as opening the door for someone. I finish my journaling by asking what I learned today, what I did well today and what am I going to do with what I learned today.

I'm now in a good frame of mind and ready for bed.

D. Getting your sleep.

Fear is the enemy of sleep. Therefore, you want to do anything you can to have a good night's sleep. I spend about five minutes meditating when I get into bed.

Sometimes I fall asleep during the meditation. I then visualize the next day going exactly as I planned it. Maybe I'll visualize a long-term goal or the nice vacation I'm going to take.

I'll then meditate some more until I fall asleep. The challenge, at least for me, wasn't falling asleep but getting back to sleep, when I wake up in the middle of the night.

My trick? You guessed it. Meditation. That's what works for me.

E. Find someone you can unload on (hint, it's not your wife or husband).

It's really hard being the spouse of the CEO, so you can't come home and just dump on your spouse. However, you do need to get your feelings out.

It can't be your board of directors, because you will scare them. Instead, you should have a trusted advisor, friend, or confidant who you can talk to.

The person needs to be someone you know will always act in your best interest.

F. Taking a walk during the day helps too.

You can't just be in the office all day, if you're feeling the fear. I used to enjoy going for a walk during lunch with just me and my thoughts. Sometimes, I would call my advisor or coach.

Now, I saved one of my favorites for last.

G. You can just get out and sell.

Do you want to remind yourself of why you're doing what you're doing? Visit some customers. Then, win some business. Nothing eliminates fear like winning business.

Winning business triggers many positive emotions. Winning business helps you dig in and fight even harder for your business.

Winning business also helps you to dance with the

fear.

You're going to feel fear as an entrepreneur. You will, and the fear is likely to stay with you through your journey. You may never get rid of the fear of failure, but you can learn to live with it.

Try meditating, having a morning routine, a night-time routine, getting your sleep, a trusted confidant you can talk to, taking walks and selling.

What is the One Trait That All Successful Entrepreneurs Have?

W e were literally down to our last dollar. In fact, truth be told, we didn't even have a dollar.

Times were so tough, that every week I had to get down on my hands and knees and beg our investors for enough money to cover payroll and basic expenses.

It was humiliating. It was painful beyond belief. It was also absolutely what I had to do.

Maybe it was the time, early in my company's existence, when my two cofounders "Jim" and "John" quit the company right before we were about to be funded. Jim and John then stole the company's IP (down to the slide deck we were using to raise money) and left me for dead.

It may have been the time the Great Recession hit right in the middle of our initial fundraising efforts. Silicon Valley was effectively shut down for almost a year. However, somehow, we had to make it through the abyss.

Maybe it was the time when one of our investors blocked every term sheet we received for reasons to this day I don't fully understand. The investor was literally cutting his own throat. We had no money, and it looked like we were going to have to shut the company down.

It could have also been the time when one of our manufacturing partners had a quality problem that potentially was going to stop us from shipping.

Or maybe....

Okay. Enough already. You get the idea.

There are many things that stand in the way of a startup's success. There are also many things that stand in the way of you succeeding in life.

The only things that gets you through the tough times are determination, belief and (most importantly) grit.

Why is grit so important?

You will not get through the tough times without grit. There are always tough times running a startup.

What is grit?

Grit is the passion and perseverance to achieve your goals over a very long time. Grit is stamina. Grit is living life like it is a marathon and not a sprint.

Grit is getting back up, every time that you are knocked down. Every single time.

The defining moment for my "grittiness" came during my junior year of college.

I was an Electrical Engineering major. There were roughly 200 of us at the beginning of my junior year in college.

The first quarter was the toughest. We had four EE courses, that were back to back every Tuesday and Thursday:

Third Year Calculus. I still remember it today. The course was taught by Dr. Lewak. It was the weed-out course.

Stochastic Processes. This beauty was taught by Dr. Helstrom. My memory of this course is that it was very theoretical...and tough.

Analog IC Design. Taught by Dr. Coles. This was my favorite class, but it wasn't easy. Coles was tough.

Queuing Theory. I can't remember who the teacher was. It was another theoretical course.

The worst part was that each course had homework due every Tuesday. It meant you usually didn't sleep Monday night.

All-nighters were the norm during my junior year. It was nothing a lot of coffee and No-doze wouldn't cure.

Oh, and I haven't even gotten to the tests. The tests were brutal.

I remember in my senior year giving copies of my tests, with my answers, to a junior. The scores were in the range of 40% or so.

"Dude," the junior said to me. "I'm sorry."

Little did he know that those were some of the best scores in the class! Thank goodness the tests were graded on a curve, or everyone would have failed.

I grew my hair really long and I had a beard. I remember calling my Mom before I came home for Thanksgiving and telling her, "Mom, I have a beard."

"Shave it!" Mom said to me.

I didn't shave my beard or cut my hair.

My mantra was, "I can do anything, if I can get through this."

It was brutal. However, I did it. Of the original 200 EE students starting my junior year, only 60 of us made it through.

I also knew, after my junior year in college, that I could do anything I choose to do in life. I didn't call it grit back then, but I knew I could grind with the best of them.

What are the keys to developing grit?

The great thing about grit is that it doesn't require you have great intellect. Grit is all about doing the same things over and over again.

Even when you don't have hope, you keep going.

Even when you don't want to, you keep going.

For example, Blossom and I like to go on runs together. There are some mornings where one of us or both of us really don't have the energy.

I looked at Blossom after one particularly tough run. I asked, panting, "How'd you do?"

"It was really tough, but I made it. It's days like today that make it possible to have easy running days."

Blossom has grit.

How do you develop grit?

Here are the tricks I use:

A. Have a plan and stick to it. You need a plan to know where you're going. It doesn't have to be complicated, but you need a plan.

B. Have a daily schedule. My plan becomes my daily schedule. I don't like to do lists, so I use my calendar to plan my day. I find it keeps me focused throughout the day.

Hint: Give yourself some short breaks between

tasks. You'll find it easier to get everything done, so you feel good at the end of the day.

C. Set small incremental goals to achieve. Kaizen is a really powerful tool that I now just began using. It's the art of setting small goals.

This doesn't mean you don't also have big goals. However, you can use the small goals as stepping-stones to the big goals. Try it.

D. Celebrate your successes, no matter how small. The celebrations don't have to be big. Maybe go to the movies with your spouse. How about a cup of coffee or you could buy yourself that new book? Just celebrate.

E. Don't quit, if things don't go your way. Not everything is going to work out the way you want. Just don't give up. Keep moving. Learn from your mistakes.

F. Visualize your success. Maybe I should have put visualization first. It's another great tool that I've recently learned.

I visualize the day ahead going exactly like I want it to every night before I go to bed. I also visualize the day ahead going exactly like I want it to when I wake up in the morning.

The one thing you can't be taught....

I can't think of another way to say it. It is resolve.

It's this ability to get up, every time you get knocked down.

Even when you don't feel like getting up...

Even when you're bone tired...

Even when you're down to your last dollar...

Even when you've lost hope...

Just get up. That's grit.

You'll know you've got grit, when you can just get up.

What Were The 17 Biggest Surprises When You Founded Your Company?

I remember talking with Jeroen, my fellow co-founder and VP of Engineering, after we'd been working together for about one year. Jeroen smiled at me and said, "I'm in line at the market and I just want everyone to start moving faster!

"That used to never happen to me."

Then we both laughed.

The key is recognizing that you are changing. You want everything to move at the same fast speed your company is moving at: FAST!

However, remember to not lose your patience with your spouse and your family.

Here are 17 other crazy and surprising things that you'll likely go through when you start your company.

A. Every word you speak matters.

Congratulations. I don't know whether you realized it, but you are now an actor.

Your stage is your office.

Let me give you an example.

I was in my office late one Friday afternoon. We had our company meeting during lunch earlier in the day.

Jeroen walked into my office and said, "One of my guys was worried because you frowned when you answered the question about revenue."

"I frowned?" I said. "I don't remember frowning."

"Yes, he thought you frowned. So he thought things were really bad."

I was laughing at this point.

This anecdote just shows you how everything you say, everything you do, every gesture you make and every email you send will all be scrutinized over and over by your team.

Your team will look for meaning, where there is none. They will wonder why you left the office at 4:30 PM.
That is why you are now an actor. You are literally on stage every second. You don't have the luxury of even taking a second off.

B. No, the market doesn't immediately notice you exist.

I think one of the most jarring things for me, was

how difficult it is to build a following and a brand for your business. What makes it even more jarring, in my case, is…

I knew going in that was going to be hard. Yet I was still surprised at how hard it is.

You'll be ecstatic the first time you get 100 visitors to your website in one day.

You'll be overjoyed the first time you get a customer. You'll truly understand why restaurant owners frame that first dollar bill they get.

C. Getting to $1M/Year in revenue is really, really hard.

I had built several businesses from $0 to greater than $100 million, before I started my company. Therefore, I had pretty high expectations that getting to $100 million was the goal.

Little did I know how unbelievably hard getting to just $1 million/year would be.
You underestimate everything when you start a company. You'll underestimate how much money you need, and you'll underestimate how difficult it is building a brand.

Therefore, is it any wonder that you'll be surprised at how difficult it is getting just $1 million/year in revenue? It shouldn't be, but it is.

D. It's hand-to-hand combat, when you're trying to

win a big deal.

Martin, one of our best engineers, said to me, "It's hand-to-hand combat getting a big customer to buy your products."

Martin was right. It can be very difficult getting big customers to buy your products.

Think about it: All your competitors want that business too! That is why it usually is a better choice for startups to go after underserved markets that might be a little smaller.

E. Hiring a great VP of Sales is unbelievably hard...

Hiring a great VP of Sales is also unbelievably important.

We cycled through three VPs of Sales in four years.

Our first VP of Sales was a co-founder who would have been great, but he just didn't have the energy and drive necessary to do the job.

Our second VP of Sales just wasn't strong enough. He tried really hard, but family issues derailed him.

Our third VP of Sales came highly recommended, but he was the wrong guy.

Why were we so inept, when it came to find a great VP of Sales?

I have to step up and take the blame. I was the CEO who hired all three VPs of Sales.

The reality is that a really great VP of Sales is not going to be interested in working at your startup, until you get to some level of scale. The job isn't meaty enough for a great VP of Sales, and it's not worth the challenge.

Therefore, you're better off without a VP of Sales, until you get to scale. That was a big surprise.

F. Expect some sort of power play every single time you are about to close your funding.

One of the saddest things to me about my experience building our company, was the drama around each fundraising event. I don't mean the external drama of dealing with investors, because you expect there to be drama dealing with investors.

I mean the unexpected internal drama of dealing with employees and co-founders leveraging the fundraising to attempt to get various things (usually more money or power).

For example, two of my co-founders (one was a friend for over 20 years) demanded that I create an "Office of the President" with them or they would quit. All major decisions would be agreed to by the three of us.

I refused, and they backed down.

"I'll quit if I don't get what I want," is the threat. Your answer always has to be no, after listening to their grievance.

It will take all of your skill not to give in, because losing a key employee before you close funding could cause you to lose your funding. I know it Is tough, but you have to find a way through the abyss.

G. Your investors likely will have surprisingly little sense of urgency over you closing your funding.

You've just signed a term sheet. You've been raising money for close to a year and funds are really low.

You want to get the money into your bank account as fast as possible, before your new investor changes their mind. Your new investor is excited to get started putting their money to work.

There are millions of dollars at stake, but your existing investors move like snails. You have closing documents that need their attention and they delay signing.

A day goes by and then another day goes by, before they sign the documents.

All this time you are sweating bullets to get your funding closed. That is the sad reality that you are the only one with a sense of urgency to close your funding.

H. That's when (and why) you need to become a polite pest.

You have to follow up on every detail with every

investor to get the round closed. You must make the extra call to the lawyers. You also have to send the extra email to nudge your investors along.

I. You're likely to learn what the "zone of insolvency" means.

Have you ever heard of the zone of insolvency? Sounds kind of like the twilight zone, doesn't it?

The zone of insolvency is when your company has more liabilities than assets. In other words, you don't have the ability to pay your bills.

You are likely to enter the zone of insolvency as you come close to closing your funding. Your attorney will make a big deal about entering the zone of insolvency.

Your investors will just shrug their shoulders. "So what, we've been there before. It's nothing to worry about," they'll say.

You'll worry, however, because it's an indication of how close to the edge your company truly is. The scary thing is it will not take much to tip it over to the point of no return.

J. You'll learn that 409A valuations are a joke.

You probably never heard of a 409A valuation before you started your company. It involves hiring an external person to determine the value of your company.

Your attorney will likely start pushing for a 409A valuation a of couple years after you launch your company, because the common wisdom is that you need a way of setting the strike price of stock options.

Your initial option price is usually arbitrarily set at around $0.12 per share. Why? It is because everyone else's option price is around $0.12 per share.

However, as you get bigger, you can't just go with an arbitrary number anymore, can you? It makes sense, until the valuation of your options suddenly jumps from $0.12 to $1.12.

Oops.

Your new hires are pissed because the exercise price on their stock options is now a large number. You want to keep that number low, so your employees can make more money.

Therefore, you nudge your independent expert to come up with a lower valuation of your company. "Ah, that's better," you say to yourself, when you see the new price of $0.17 per share.

K. You'll find out your team is more resilient than you think.

One of the more surprising things you'll likely learn is how resilient your team really is. I did.

The way you build up your team's resilience is

through transparency. Share with your team the bad stuff, as well as the good stuff.

You'll likely be surprised at the positive response your team has to adversity.

One word of caution before you lay your soul bare: Never show your fear or panic about what's going on, however bad it is.

You want to appear to be in control (remember that you are an actor), even if you're scared to death.

L. Your investors expect you to screw up...

...especially if you are a first time CEO.

I'll never forget listening to some of the partners at the VC fund, where I was an Entrepreneur in Residence (EIR), talk about first time CEOs.

"Of course, the CEO is going to make hundreds of mistakes," was the consensus view.

Your investors are expecting you to make mistakes. However, there are three things you need to remember if and when you make mistakes:

Never surprise your investors. In other words, don't hide your mistake from your investors, and...

Tell your investors about problems, before you have a board meeting. Your investors will then not be surprised by the problem in front of the other board members. And...

Learn from each mistake. Then you will not repeat the mistakes, and you'll get smarter.

M. You really do have to be 100X better than your closest competitor to win.

You're a small startup. The world has existed quite well without you and your company. The only way to cut through the noise, is to be significantly better than your competitors.

I learned this one the hard way:

Our first products that were maybe 30% better than the competition didn't sell well, and...

Our second-generation products were 3X to 10X better and they sold well, but...

Our third-generation products were 100X better and groundbreaking and they really sold well!

N. You will be obsessing about your company every waking moment.

You're on vacation with your family, and what are you thinking about? The company!

You're going for a run on a Saturday, and what are you thinking about? The company!

You're at the movies and what are you thinking about? The company!

Your obsession with your company never goes

away, even while you're sleeping.

O. Your investors trust you more than you realize.

"They're actually going to wire $12 million into our bank account," I said to myself.

We had just completed the "documents" phase of our initial funding. We had signed all the paperwork. Here were these people that we barely knew about to wire us $12 million.

I don't know if it counts as a surprise, but it shows you the trust that your investors are putting in you. Your investors know you may fail. Your investors also know you may lose all their money.

However, your investors are willing to wire you millions of dollars. They expect you to figure the rest out for yourself.

Is that crazy or what?

P. You'll likely never, ever, ever want to work for anyone again.

Maybe this isn't such a big surprise, but it certainly was confirmed for me after I sold my company.

I had no desire. In fact, I had negative desire to work for anyone ever again.

I just couldn't stand the thought of working for anyone. I'd rather starve than work for someone again.

That's why it's so hard for ex-CEOs to become VPs.

Potential employers know you don't want to work for them either.

Q. You will have people you trust turn on you, but...

You will have people you didn't expect to help you time and time again.

We already spoke of the betrayal (see answer F). However, you'll be amazed at the support you get in surprising places.

An example is the entry-level engineer who stayed all night fulfilling sample requests without being asked.

R. You will never be closer to another group of people again in your career.

Building a company from the ground up is an intense experience. You go through many things and it is very intense.

A bond forms between you and your team that will be there forever. That is why building a company is so special and so enjoyable.

For all the problems, late nights and near-death experiences, it's the feeling that you and your team are doing something really special together. Nobody is going to get in your way.

What Is the One and Only One Key To Being A Great CEO?

I've come to a conclusion in the past few weeks. It's a stunner. At least it is to me.

What is my conclusion you ask?

I've concluded that I'm a horrible manager. I am maybe the worst manager ever.

Okay. Maybe horrible is too strong a word.

Maybe ineffective would be a better way to describe things.

How did I come to the conclusion that I'm an ineffective manager?

I have an over 20-year track record of never being able to rescue and turn around an employee that is failing. 100% failure. Every. Single. Time.

My attempts at saving employees have been incredible flops.

Take the case of "Tom." Tom was an applications engineer, who I inherited when I took over a new division at the company I just joined.

Tom was smart and capable. However, Tom just didn't seem motivated.

I, therefore, spent extra time with Tom to help him out.

I tutored Tom. I repeatedly asked him if anything was wrong. "Nope. Nothing is wrong," was his reply.

"Tom, you do understand you need to get this work done by Monday?"

"Yes, I do," was always his response.

Monday would roll around and the work wasn't done.

"Why didn't the work get done?"

"I ran out of time."

"Why didn't you ask for help?"

"I don't need help."

I tried reducing Tom's workload. The results remained the same.

I went out for lunch one day. There was a note taped to my computer, when I returned.

"I QUIT!"

Tom had quit with no notice.

My perfect record of failure stayed intact. I still had never successfully turned around an employee.

There was the case of Gary.

Gary was a super nice guy who we hired into sales. He had a good track record.

However, Gary wasn't hitting the numbers that he set for himself. He was going to fail, unless we were able to help him.

"I'll work directly with Gary," I told our VP of Sales.

It was the kiss of death.

I tried helping Gary every way that I could think of. Gary's results continued to be poor.

We would have no choice but to let Gary go.

My perfect record of management failure stayed intact. Again. Do you want to be a great CEO? Hire great employees!

That's it. It's so simple too!

In other words:

- Just hire great employees

- Pay these great employees a fair wage.

- Put them in an environment where they can succeed.

- Stay out of these great employees' way.

- Coach and guide them, when they ask for

help or need help.

This is why recruiting and hiring great people is the most important role you have as a CEO.

Maybe I'm just horrible at saving employees that are failing. However, even if you are good at saving employees, aren't you better off if you just hire really great employees to start with?

Think about it:

- Great employees do the right thing.

- Great employees require a minimal amount of management.

- Best of all, great employees contribute beyond their job descriptions.

- Great employees scale, as your company scales.

- Great employees stick around for the long run, assuming that you pay them fairly and promote them when they should be promoted.

It is very simple. All you need to do is just get out of the way!

This involves creating the collaborative environment great employees need to thrive.

The cost of not recruiting a great team is extreme:

- Your team doesn't execute as well as you want.

- You spend more of your time on lower level issues.

- You spend too much time fixing personnel issues (you'll spend enough time on personnel issues with a great team).

- You don't devote the time you need to the long-term future of your company.

- Your results are not what you want them to be.

Let me give you an example.

I'm working with an entrepreneur named "Peter." Peter has built his business up to $4M/year, but his company's growth has hit a wall.

Sometimes you have to change your team, because you are changing strategies. The problem, in Peter's case, was the quality of the team.

We started talking about Peter's direct reports. I asked Peter a simple question:
"Imagine your organization one year from now. Who of your senior managers fits in that future organization, and who of your senior managers doesn't fit in that future organization?"

Two of Peter's six senior managers didn't fit.

"What are you going to do?" I asked Peter.

"I'm going to see if they can scale up. What do you think?"

"I don't think it's realistic to expect your team to scale up, based on what I've heard."

I told Peter about my perfect track record of failure in turning around problem employees.

Peter had five senior managers that reported directly to him. I asked Peter how many of his team he felt would fit his vision of where he wanted the company to go.

Peter said only two of his five senior managers would fit his vision for his company.

Ouch.

You can't execute the changes you need, if you don't have the right team around you.

Peter is going to have to recruit a new team and change strategies at the same time. From experience, I know Peter's results will continue suffering, until he is working with a great team.

Imagine if Peter had the right team? Peter and his team could then move quickly to change the company.

It always comes back to your team.

Always.

I started thinking about the successful teams that I had built. In each case, the quality of the people I was working with was really strong.

What was my part in their success? The most important thing I did was recruiting the team.

Then, for the most part, I got out of the great team's way.

A very wise man told me early in my career, "You can't be a manager, if you can't recruit."

Do you want to be a great CEO? Then recruit and build a great team.

What is the Brutal Truth About Being A Startup CEO?

It's 7:35 AM and cold in the office.

I turn on the lights, because I am the first person in the building. I walk into my office, plug in my computer and I take a sip of my Starbucks.

They got the milk to coffee ratio just right in my latte this morning. It tastes extra good.

I look at my email and answer any urgent questions from overnight, then I get to work.

I have maybe an hour to an hour and a half before the day is not mine anymore. Starting at 9 AM, the next eight to nine hours will be meeting after meeting after meeting.

I've got to be focused right now on what I need to get done.

I get to work.

This is my time. It is my time to be creative and to add value. Therefore, I start working on the things only I can do.

I'm on a roll. My pace quickens.

I start tapping the keys on my keyboard faster and harder. It is as if the strength of my keystrokes will make a difference. LOL.

The rest of the world has gone away. I'm in flow.

The phone rings. I look at the number, and it's one of our investors calling.

We're raising money (when aren't you?), so I take the call.

The call turned out to be about nothing important, so I get back to work. However, the flow is broken. Now it's 8:50 AM, and the team is starting to arrive in the office.

In another hour, the buzz will be in full effect. If you've ever been at a company that's got momentum, then you know what I mean.

It's that buzz of energy. You can just feel it. I love that feeling, because you feel like you can conquer the world.

Tina knocks on my door. "Brett, I'm sorry, but can you authorize this payment."

That's it. My day is over.

I sign the authorization, and then I go to the first meeting of the day. It's the engineering review meeting.

It is going to last two hours. Jeroen asked me to

come this morning, because he wants me to back him up on how important it is that we stay on schedule.

And so it goes...

That's the first brutal truth about being CEO. You have less time to do the things you want than you realize.

Every day is a struggle between what your team needs (or wants) you to do, and what you want to do. Some days, you take the bait and you end up spending more time than you should on helping the team.

There are other days when you just shut the door and focus on what you need to get done.

It's a delicate balance.

You can't just do what you want every day, because you have to help guide the rest of the company. However, if you spend so much time guiding the company, you don't get what you need to do done.

That leads to...

The second brutal truth about being CEO. You're all alone with no one to talk to.

You can't talk to your co-founders about what's worrying you. There's too much risk they might tell the team.

You also can't talk to your investors about what's worrying you. There's too much risk that your investors will worry in the wrong way.

You can't talk to your spouse about what's worrying you. There's too much risk you'll overwhelm your spouse.

There's literally no one you can confide in. No one. This is where a good mentor or coach comes in handy.

However, there is one brutal truth that outshines all the other brutal truths about being CEO...

This brings us to the third brutal truth about being CEO. For all the problems and all the worries you have as CEO, it is the most awesome job in the world.

There wasn't a day I had as CEO that I would trade for the best day I had as an employee. There is not one. That includes the worst day ever.

Where else in the universe can you get to work with the team that you handpicked to do the job, help them get the job done and watch your team succeed?

Where else in the universe can you get to see your creation take flight, and watch customers buy your product(s) in ever increasing frequency.

Where else in the universe can you engineer exactly

the company that you want and the culture for that company?

There's no rush like it in the world.

ROUND 2: YOU HAVE A GREAT IDEA, NOW WHAT?

What Are the Three Reasons Your Startup Will Succeed?

Marc Andreessen wrote an excellent blog post about why startups succeed. His view is, when you look at the three key components to success (team, product and market), that the market is the most important reason that a startup succeeds.

Andreessen quotes what he calls "Rachleff's law," named after venture capitalist Andy Rachleff. Rachleff's law goes as follows:

- When a great team meets a lousy market, market wins.

- When a lousy team meets a great market, market wins.

- When a great team meets a great market, something special happens.

I agree with Rachleff's law. You do need to pick a great market to win. There's no doubt about it.

Rachleff's law is an investor's view of why startups succeed. Here's my view as an entrepreneur of what it takes to succeed:

A. You need a great market to go after.

I don't care how good you and your team are, an unforgiving market will kill your chances of success. This leads to my second rule of startup success.

B. You need a great team.

Great teams find great markets. Great teams pivot, when they attack an unforgiving market.

Great teams don't give up, when they are faced with obstacles. They use their grit to persevere.

The good news is you are completely in control of the team that you build. Therefore, aim high and choose great co-founders and great team members that fit and will positively add to your company culture.

This leads to my third rule of startup success.

C. You need great investors.

Every company has investors. This includes bootstrapped companies, where you're investing your own funds.

You will fail, if you if there is a mismatch between you and your investors. In fact, investor mismatch is the most difficult thing for an entrepreneur to overcome.

You are in deep trouble, if an investor decides to pull their support because you will have to scramble to find funding. Some companies make it through, but many excellent companies are killed through no fault of their own, when an investor pulls their support.

Choose your investors wisely.

This is because a great team going after a great market with supportive investors is unstoppable.

Why Do You Need Fanatical Co-founders?

I'm in the middle of reading Phil Knight's (the founder of Nike) great autobiography "Shoe Dog." I'm actually listening to the book on Audible, and I'm transfixed.

I'm about halfway through Shoe Dog. I can't stop reading/listening. In fact, I'm going to go for a run once I'm done writing this post, so I can listen some more.

It's clear from what I've read of Shoe Dog, that Knight had REALLY motivated people around him. These REALLY motivated people were critical to Nike's success.

What did Phil Knight do to motivate his team? Did he:

Have a unique quota system?

Have a unique incentive scheme?

Rely on Kaizen or other motivational techniques?

Knight did none of that. In fact, Knight's "plan" was non-existent.

It was almost as if Knight managed, by not managing at all. He just kept out of the way of the REALLY motivated team around him.

Knight's founding team was a motley crew. Bowerman, Johnson, Woodell, Hollister and the rest were certainly not out of central casting.

However, as you read Shoe Dog, you knew they were the right group for Knight.

There was a word that was rattling around in my head about Knight's founding team, but I couldn't find it.

Then, at about the halfway point of the book, Knight said the word about an early team member:

The team member was "fanatical."

Boom! Fanatical is the perfect word to describe a great co-founder. You can't stop with just your co-founders. You need everyone that joins your company early on to be a fanatic.

Let me go even one step further: You need fanatics at every stage of your company's life.

I started thinking about the successful and unsuccessful teams that I'd been involved with during my career. Were the successful teams fanatical?

I was very fortunate, early in my career, to work at Maxim Integrated Products. I watched and helped

Maxim grow to over $1 billion/year in revenue.

Maxim, like Nike, had an interesting cast of characters. However, just like Nike, the team was truly committed to the company's success. (Interestingly enough, Maxim's original campus in Portland, Oregon was right across the street from Nike.)

It was clear and obvious:

The successful teams that I'd worked with, were fanatical about the company/cause. The unsuccessful teams looked at their work like just that: work.

You're either working with the right people or you aren't.

I started my company with four co-founders. Adolfo and Jeroen were fanatical about our success. It became obvious over time that "Ken" and "Randy" were not fanatical about our success.

Ken and Randy were smart and experienced, but they didn't have that hunger and desire that you need in a startup.

The challenge with co-founders, is you many times don't know if the co-founder will work out. However, the warning signs that things will not work out are there, if you look.

Ken ran sales for us. I knew we were in trouble when Ken bought a condo in the nicest building in San Francisco.

Blossom and I had dinner one night with Ken and some friends. One of our friends, who lived in the same building Ken did, described Ken as "The Mayor."

"Everyone in the building knows Ken," my friend remarked.

Ken was going to have to be on the road a lot. Was Ken really going to want to spend weeks on end in hotel rooms away from his beautiful new home?

Ken was gone within a year.

Randy pushed to be COO. Does a five-person company really need a COO?

Randy's ego grab for title was a harbinger of other interpersonal issues he would have with other team members.

Randy was gone six months after we started.

Fanatical team members are all in.

Just like the characters that Knight worked with, Adolfo and Jeroen never complained. They just got it done.

Interestingly, neither Adolfo nor Jeroen were extroverts. Personality doesn't matter, because fanatics come in all shapes and sizes.

Most importantly, fanatical co-founders don't back

away when you have trouble. Unless you're really fortunate, your startup is going to have a near death experience or two or three.

Reading Shoe Dog, it's clear from Knight's experience building Blue Ribbon Sports (the original name for Nike for the first seven years of their existence) that Nike/Blue Ribbon had several near-death experiences. Knight's core team never once backed down.

There was one more thing that is even more important than Knight's team being all in:

Knight was all in from the start. And you, the CEO, are going to have to be all in too.

Therefore, ask yourself: Are you fanatical about your company?

You don't need to worry about motivating any co-founders, unless you are fanatical about your company. The fanatics you need to build your company will not follow you, unless you are also fanatical.

Your task is simply finding other fanatics.

Then you will never have to worry about motivation again.

You never have worry about motivating fanatics, because fanatics are self-motivated.

There are things you can do to hurt the motivation of the fanatical team you've built:

- You can micromanage them, and...

- You can not delegate to your team, and...

- You can not give your team clear goals to shoot for, and...

- You can not be transparent with your team, and...

- You can hire people that don't fit, so...

- Start with people that are fanatical about your company. You want people that will run through walls, like the group that Phil Knight had.

You will then have a fanatical team that is highly motivated.

How do you find fanatics for your team?

I was interviewing a very promising engineering candidate. Jeroen, our VP Engineering, loved the guy. The technical team loved this guy. He fit well with the company culture.

I was the final interviewer, the closer, so to speak.

We started talking, and I loved this guy too. I knew he would be a great addition to the team. We talked a little bit about the offer he was going to receive.

It was a good offer. The salary would be at market rate, and the equity was good for his level.

Then, he said, "I'm trying to calculate what type of return I'm going get if I join, versus staying at my existing company. I need to build a spreadsheet to determine the odds."

I knew right then, that he would not be joining our company.

You see, I'd met him before. Not him, but I'd met hundreds like him; the "I'm going to determine what the most likely outcome" candidate.

Fanatics don't care about the odds of success.

Every single person I ever interviewed that tried to determine the odds of success versus staying at their corporate jobs stayed at their corporate jobs.

The low odds didn't stop me from trying to get this great candidate to join the company. I did everything I could do to get him to join, but, in the end, he didn't join.

Here's the thing:

You either believe or you don't. If you believe, you take the risk, knowing that there is a high likelihood you will fail.

That is okay because you believed in what you were doing. In other words, you are a fanatic, and fanatics don't give up when the odds are stacked against them, and...

- Fanatics believe that even when all hell is breaking loose, they will find a way., and...

- Fanatics find other fanatics that are willing to break through walls just like them, and...

- Fanatics keep climbing the mountain, delaying gratification, day after day, month after month and year after year.

You have to be willing to accept the risk of complete failure, if you decide to start a company.

You may not be that type of person. That is perfectly okay. The odds are that you will be better off financially, by staying at your current job.

However, you'll never know what it's like to build something from scratch. You'll never know the joy of being part of a great team of fanatics that pulled off the impossible.

This is reason why, despite the odds being stacked against you, that you start a company.

How Much Equity Do Your Employees Deserve?

I was advising the two founders of a technology company. They had no funding, and they were looking to hire a VP of Engineering.

They found a good candidate for the position. However, they only wanted to give him 1% equity vesting over four years. I told them that the candidate wasn't going to take the risk of joining for such a small percentage ownership.

Their answer was, "Why not? We're going to be worth $1B in a couple of years."

Therein lies the problem:

Many entrepreneurs overvalue their equity and get very stingy in the process.

It seems to me there that are two types of founders:

A. The "Spread the Wealth Founders," where the founders are very generous with equity, or...

B. The "Stingy, we are in it Only for Ourselves Founders," where they grudgingly give out equity.

You either get it regarding equity or you don't get

it.

We've all watched Shark Tank where, seemingly every week, an entrepreneur fights to keep every single percent of his or her equity. Ask yourself this question:

"Does it really matter whether you have 80% or 90% ownership?"

You're thinking, "Of course, it matters. I've just lost 10% ownership."

Of course, you're right. However, what if you are hurting your chances of success? What if 80% ownership is worth a lot more than 90% ownership? Would you still want to hold onto that extra 10%?

It turns out that being stingy with equity hurts your chances of success. Therefore, the "Spread the Wealth Founders" have a much better chance of success. Noam Wasserman wrote about this phenomenon in a 2008 HBR article titled, *The Founder's Dilemma.* Wasserman states:

"Choosing money: A founder who gives up more equity to attract investors builds a more valuable company than one who parts with less—and ends up with a more valuable slice, too."

Wasserman isn't the only one who believes spreading the wealth is the right way to go. Andy Ratchleff, former venture capitalist and current founder of Wealthfront, believes that one of the common traits of successful startups is spreading the wealth. Ratchleff says in his article, *The Right Way to Grant Equity to Your Employees:*

"When I was a venture capitalist, I noticed companies that seldom lost employees due to recruitment had a lot in common. Sure, they offered challenging and inspiring work environments sought by top-tier talent. But you might be surprised to learn they all rewarded outstanding performance through the issuance of additional stock options (or as is now the case, RSUs) in a similar way."

I worked at a company years ago, where the CEO, "Bob," threw equity around like manhole covers. Bob owned a huge amount of the company and controlled the board of directors.

The company had significant structural problems. Many executives (myself included) proposed plans that would have changed the fortunes of the company.

Bob wouldn't listen. He wanted control. He was going to do things his way.

It took years, but eventually the investors forced him out.

That is the founder's dilemma that Wasserman is talking about:

- Yes, it feels great to have all the power, and…

- Yes, it feels great to be able to do exactly what you want to do, but...

- You can develop a pretty mean case of hubris if you're not careful, and...

- Hubris will likely kill you and your company.

Being CEO can be really tricky. Everyone is kowtowing to you. Everyone is telling you that you are great. Everyone is telling you that you're right.

It's difficult not to be affected. I know.

On the other hand, you likely were told by just about everyone that your new company was not going to succeed, you'd never get funding and you were making a huge mistake. I was told all of this and more.

As a result, your desire to keep control of the company is understandable. However, holding on to every percent of equity, tooth and nail, is likely not going to give you the result you want for you and your company.

Here's what I'm not saying:

- I'm not saying you should give away equity like candy, and...

- I'm not saying you should overpay your employees, however...

- I am saying you should be fair because…:

- Fairness builds loyalty, and…

- Fairness builds a great team, and most importantly…

- Fairness gives you the best return on your investment.

Yes, you may give up more equity than you like, but you will be better off.

I'll never forget a conversation I had with one of our investors, when we were closing the initial round of funding for my company. He said to me:

"Brett, the amount of equity you have in the company today is irrelevant. I can tell you already that the investors are going to end up with X and the company is going to end up with Y.

"The rest of it doesn't matter."

I always felt that what he was really saying was, "There's a fair outcome for both of us, and that's what I'm committed to." Now, having said that, we had another investor whose goal was to squeeze every percentage of equity he could from us like blood from a stone.

What is the right amount of equity to relinquish?

There is no one size fits all answer. However, let me give you the thought process I follow:

A. If winning means giving up more equity, then I am all for giving up more equity.

B. You know you have given the right equity to someone, when you feel good about the amount and the employee feels good about the amount.

There are many articles on the Internet about equity allocation for different positions. You can use these as a guide. You can also network with other entrepreneurs to find out what they are doing. Your investors should have research on equity allocation, so you can use this as another resource.

Oh, before I forget, make sure that the equity grants you give vest over time:

- A typical equity grant should vest over four years, and…
- The first 25% should vest after twelve months (a one year "cliff"), and…

- The remaining 75% should vest monthly in 36 equal increments.

This structure protects you, just in case someone doesn't work out. You then haven't given away a large chunk of your company to someone who isn't contributing.

One final thing that you should do: refresh the stock options of your team.

You and your team are going to be diluted, as you

raise more money. That's a fact of life. However, you want to keep your team motivated. The way to do this, is by refreshing their stock options.

This means giving your employees an additional stock grant when a round of funding closes. This is especially important, if the dilution was significant.

You will want to increase your option pool to grant your employees new options. You may be surprised to hear this, but your investors will likely support you.

You measure how much new stock to give by how much ownership a certain position should have, based on the life and timing of the company. Let's say you just raised your Series B funding.

An employee in a certain position was initially given 0.6% ownership initially. The employee has 0.35% after Series B closed but should be at 0.5%. You should grant the employee another set of options for 0.15% ownership.

You should always be fair: someone who took the risk of joining early, should be rewarded for taking that risk.

I always used to tell prospective new hires that if I hire you today, you are going to own more of the company than your clone, if I hire your clone a year from now. Refreshing is crucial to fairness.

Refreshing is also a key retention tool. We live in a competitive world.

You are going to lose your employees to the competition, if you don't compensate them fairly. Your investors know this and they should be supportive. However, this is only if you are being fair, not greedy.

What happened with the entrepreneurs you were advising?

The guys I was advising never got it. I realized they were never going to win. Therefore, I did what I would advise you to do, if you were in the same situation: Be gracious and move on.

More importantly, we can learn that holding onto every percentage of equity is not the way to increase your chances of success.

Your approach should be fair and generous. In return, you will likely be rewarded with a loyal team of motivated employees.

A loyal, motivated team will increase the chances of your company's success, and a loyal, motivated team will increase the value of your equity.

What Does the Role Of COO Look Like In A Startup?

Nonexistent.

Take it from someone who had a COO co-founder, you don't need a COO when you're starting a company.

I added a COO as a co-founder to my company. "Randy" was talented, had tons of experience and knowledge, and he helped me secure funding.

There was just one little problem with having a Chief Operations Officer in a startup, especially an early stage startup. And that problem is...

Startups, especially early stage startups, don't need a Chief Operations Officer.

Hmmm.

Let's see. What does a COO do again? Yeah, that's right. A COO manages the day to day operations of a company.

That must mean a COO needs to have good management skills, right? Sure. A COO must have to be a good manager.

However, doesn't a CEO also have to be a good manager? Of course. You'd better be a good manager, if you're a CEO.

What else does a COO need to be good at? A COO must also be able to manage multiple disciplines in a company.

However, doesn't a CEO have to be a good at managing multiple disciplines in a company? You bet. If you're going to be a successful CEO, then you'd better be good at managing multiple disciplines.

What else? What else does COO need to be good at? Leadership. A COO has to be good leader.

However, doesn't a CEO have to be a good leader too? Absolutely. You will fail as the CEO, if you're not a good leader.

So far it seems that everything a COO has to be good at, you have to be good at as a CEO.

Let's keep going and see if there's something a COO has to be good at that you don't have to be good at as CEO.

What about integrity? A COO better have integrity. Again, you are correct.

However, you'd better have even more integrity than your COO, if you're going to be a successful CEO.

How about strategic vision? A COO needs that too, right? I'm not so sure, but I'll give that one to you.

Guess what? You'd better have an even better strategic vision as CEO. Here's the reality...

If you do hire a COO at an early stage startup, it's likely to backfire on you.

One of the biggest mistakes I made, was agreeing to make my co-founder Randy COO. Randy was talented, and Randy had extensive experience. However, Randy failed as COO, and I eventually had to fire him.

What I failed to recognize, was that Randy wanted to be COO to gratify his ego. Randy was responsible for manufacturing and test engineering. We just didn't need a COO at that early stage. No company does.

A five-person company doesn't need a COO. Nor does a 20-person company need a COO. A 200-person company doesn't need a COO either.

Maybe you need a COO when you get to 1000 people.

Until you get to 1000 employees, then you shouldn't worry about hiring a COO. You can do the job, and you should do the job until then.

Every company I've worked with that had a COO when I started working with them, eventually let the COO go. The CEOs came to realize that the COO was hurting their company more than helping the company.

Once the COO was gone, the CEO was able to more effectively lead their company to success. You'll likely find the same thing also holds in your case.

A COO typically will manage part or all of the daily operations of a company. The idea is the Chief Executive Officer is now free to focus more on the long-term strategy of the company.

The problem is the CEO of a startup needs to be focused on the daily operations of the company and the strategy of the company. You, the CEO, need to be hyper-focused on the details early on in order to succeed.

You're giving someone a title they don't deserve.

I gave Randy the COO title, because he wanted the title. However, Randy hadn't earned the title of COO. All he was going to do was to manage test engineering and manufacturing.

Randy should have had the title of Vice President of Manufacturing, not COO. That would have been appropriate. Instead, I created an unnecessary ego problem.

I can't say for sure that Randy's failure was due to me naming him COO. However, I can certainly say that naming him COO didn't help. The reality is I should have waited to name Randy COO, until he earned the job.

Can you find someone who can take over some of the day to day management of the company?

If you can, that person might be your COO. That person might also be your President or Senior VP of Operations. It's really about how you want to divide the work and what titles will satisfy you and your team.

What Are The 19 Wishes That Every Founder Needs Granted?

D ear Genie in a bottle,

I'm going to start a new company. Yes, Genie. I know I'm crazy. I know I only get nineteen wishes.

Genie, I'm really going to need you at your best. So, with these nineteen wishes, please grant me:

A. A great co-founder.

Steve Jobs needed Steve Wozniak. Bill Gates needed Paul Allen. Mick needed Keith and vice versa. Every great founder needs at least one great co-founder. So, please grant me a great co-founder. And Genie, please grant me...

B. Wisdom.

Decisions are never clear, when you are CEO. There are multiple options and multiple paths.

Take the wrong path and you're dead. Take the right path and you are on your way to success.

Please grant me the wisdom to decide on the right path. And, while you're at it Genie, please grant me...

C. Grit.

I know it's a tough road to success. I know I am going to get knocked down time and again.

I'm ready for it, Genie. At least, I think I am. However, I'm going to need your help.

I'm going to need Grit and lots of it to hang in there during all the rough times ahead. Oh, and could you also grant me...

D. Patience.

I know, Genie, that patience is a dirty word when you're running a startup. Nevertheless, I'm going to need the patience to stay the course.

I can't be bouncing from one business model to another business model, for example. I'm going to need patience, the close cousin of grit, if we're going to win.

You know what I could really use Genie? I could really use...

E. A reality distortion field.

Like the one Steve Jobs had. Yeah. I think that would be really useful.

You need your team to achieve the impossible to achieve startup success. That requires you bend reality, when you're starting a new company.

Then it would really useful Genie, if you could grant me...

F. A great network.

It would allow me to recruit a great team to work with. You know. It would be a team that is passionate, has integrity, is smart and fits the company culture.

A team full of fanatics, like the one Phil Knight had at Nike, sure would do the trick.

It also wouldn't hurt, if you could introduce me to some great investors too.

Since we're on the subject of integrity, Genie please grant me...

G. A soul.

Temptation is everywhere. I never, ever want to lose my integrity. Even if it means doing things that might hurt. Even if it means, yes, that the company might go under.

Genie, I'm also going to need...

H. Generosity.

I can't expect to keep 100% of the equity for myself. I need to be fair and generous to the team.
I know that I will be rewarded many times over by being generous. Speaking of generosity, Genie

please grant me...

I. Humility.

Building a startup is a team sport Genie. I'm going to need the humility to give the praise of our success to the team, not me.

I'm also going to need the humility to accept the blame for all of our mistakes and problems. I'm the CEO, and I bear the ultimate responsibility.

Speaking of team, Genie please grant me...

J. A really strong team.

I know, Genie. We have to recruit the team with our network. However, it would be great if you could at least give us a pool of talented people to recruit. Oh, one thing that would really be helpful building a great team Genie would be...

K. H1-B Visas.

Man, oh man, do we need them, Genie. It's tough to build a great team here in the United States with home grown talent.

There are just not enough American-born engineers to fill our ranks. We need H1-B visas, so we can continue adding the best and brightest to our team.

Genie could you please grant me the wish to keep our team happy.

L. A great culture.

Culture is overlooked by many CEOs. Please don't let me overlook having a great culture. Our chances of success go way up, if we get the culture right.

I've already asked you for a lot Genie, but could you also grant me:

M. Class and Grace.

Yes Genie, class and grace. I know I'm going to have to do a lot of tough things. I know I am going to have to fire people.

I hate firing people, but I know not every person is going to work out. Yes, Genie, I know it's my fault when a person doesn't work out.

So, I need to let people go with class and grace. It's going to be really rough Genie, so please grant me:

N. A loving and supportive family.

It's going to be tough on my family because, even when I'm with them, I'm going to be focusing on the company.

There are also going to be near-death experiences, where it looks like everything we've worked for is going to go away. That's when I'm really going to need my family's love and support.

And, every once in a while, Genie please grant me:

O. A good night's sleep.

Yeah, a good night's sleep would be really nice. I know there are going to be nights where I sleep very little.

Keeping those sleepless nights to a minimum would be great. One thing that will help me sleep well Genie would be if you could grant me:

P. Good investors.

By good investors, I mean supportive investors. You know, investors that are going to hang in there during the ups and downs of building a company.

It would really make me and my investors happy Genie, if you could grant me:

Q. An exploding market.

It doesn't even have to be the market we originally aimed for Genie. It can be a new market that needs what we're developing (with a few tweaks).

A growing market would be really nice. And speaking of markets, Genie could you grant me:

R. A good competitor.

It sounds crazy Genie, but I know we're going to have competition. Therefore, why not wish for a good competitor?

I'd like a competitor that really pushes us to do our best. A competitor that fights hard but fairly.

Finally, Genie, please grant me the most important wish of all is:

S. Luck.

None of the other wishes you granted me Genie matters, if I don't have some luck. Without luck I know it's next to impossible to win, so please grant me some luck Genie. I know I'm going to need it.

Thanks Genie! I know I'm asking for a lot, but I'm going to need every bit of your help to succeed,

Brett

What Is the Hardest Part About Starting Your Own Company?

I was scared. I should have been thrilled, but I was scared.

It was Sunday night, and Monday I would officially begin my journey as an EIR (Entrepreneur in Residence) at a VC fund based in San Francisco. It was an incredible opportunity to build an Analog IC company (my expertise) with VC backing, and now I had to deliver.

I knew the playbook for building the company inside and out. After all, I'd been building companies like this for close to 20 years.

I knew the moves. Yet I was scared because, even though I knew the moves, I wasn't sure I would be able to execute on the most important move in the startup playbook: finding a great VP Engineering.

Okay. Maybe I was more worried than scared. However, it was still a daunting task. Really great VPs of Engineering just don't grow on trees.

You need to knock on a lot of doors to build your team.

So, there I was, zero days into the job, worried about finding this elusive person. I had to buy something at Fry's and I ran right into "Jim." Jim and I had worked together years ago, and I had always thought highly of him.

Jim asked me what I was up to. I told him that I was in the process of starting a company. Jim said he'd be interested in working with me on the project.

It was great that Jim was interested in working with me. However, Jim was a marketing person, not an engineering VP. I still had the same problem of finding a great VP Engineering.

Now there were two of us working on solving the problem. That meant we could leverage Jim's network of contacts, in addition to my network of contracts.

Jim suggested we meet with "John." Jim and John had worked together under my old mentor and boss, Ziya.

Jim and I had lunch with John the next week. We met at Bucks in Woodside.

As usual, Bucks was loud. And, as usual, the food was mediocre at best. Jim, John and I had a good conversation.

John and I agreed to meet again. The second meeting also went well. We talked about our philosophies about building a company like this. The good news was there was a good deal of overlap.

We also got along well, so I felt pretty good about possibly bringing John onto the team.

You always need to check your references, before you bring on a co-founder.

Jim was vouching for John, so that made me feel good. However, I wanted more confirmation.

I called Ziya up in Istanbul, where he was living. Ziya was very excited about John joining the team. I also called another CEO friend who John had worked for. He told me John was a guru.

I was sold.

John would become the third founder of our company.

You need a minimum of three months, before you know if you and your co-founders will work out.

I was thrilled because we had solved the really tough problem of finding a really great VP Engineering. John checked all the boxes.

- John could recruit.

- John could manage an engineering team.

- John was hands on and technically strong.

Everything seemed really good. All we had to do

was complete our business plan and start raising money.

Ziya flew into Silicon Valley about two months after we started, and he wanted to have dinner with us. We had a really nice dinner in Palo Alto.

I remember John saying to Ziya, "We don't always agree with each other..."

John's tone was positive, so maybe it was nothing. I still made a mental note, because we hadn't disagreed about anything.

The arguments literally started the next day. Apparently, John had been holding in his feelings about my broad vision for the company.

John wanted to focus narrowly on one specific product area which was, of course, his area of expertise. I was okay with starting in his area of expertise, but I knew, to build a big company, we needed to expand beyond this one area.

John never could get his head around the vision, so he quit and stole the company's IP in the process. Oh, and he convinced Jim to quit too.

I was back to square one.

Where was I going to find a second great VP Engineering?

I started calling everyone I could think of, and I eventually landed on "Julius." Julius also had a good reputation. After doing some quick reference checks on Julius, I added him to the team.

We were having my in-laws over for dinner one Sunday night, when I got a call from Julius. "Hi Brett, I don't know how to tell you this, but I don't think I have the energy to do a startup at this time.

"I'll help you until you find my replacement."

There was more to the conversation. A lot more in fact. We spoke for over an hour, but it was clear that I would have to find a third great VP Engineering.

How many rabbits could I pull out of one hat?

Your team is directly related to your company culture, and your company culture is the reason most startups fail.

We were already raising money, when Julius decided to bow out. I decided to keep going.

I would be the acting VP Engineering, until we found a permanent VP Engineering.

I also decided that I would be upfront and honest with potential investors about where we were at. More importantly, I decided that we would take our time, relatively, in finding the right permanent VP Engineering.

It took a long five months to find Jeroen. However, the fit was perfect, or as close to perfect as you could get, from day one.

A. You want your co-founders to share the same vision for the company.

Jeroen is incredibly mild mannered. However, underneath his calm exterior he was incredibly passionate about building the same type of company I wanted to build.

In fact, Jeroen was just as fanatical as I was about seeing our vision through. Fanaticism is a critical component that you need in your co-founders. And...

B. You want your technical VP/CTO to have good business sense.

It is not enough for your technical VP just to be strong technically. You need your technical VP to also have good business sense.

Think of it this way. You're going to need your co-founder(s) to buy into the vision for the company. You're also going to want your co-founder(s) to challenge your decisions.

What happens if your co-founder(s) challenge the wrong decisions, and they can't be convinced, despite all your best efforts, to support what you do? Inevitably, you will have problems, if there are too many disconnects between you and your co-founder(s).

Jeroen quickly became someone that I could rely on

for useful feedback on many business decisions beyond engineering. That's a huge bonus. And...

C. You want your co-founder(s) to have integrity.

Your chances of success go way down, if you have co-founders that lack integrity. It doesn't matter how brilliant they are. Without integrity you can't trust your cofounder(s). Without trust, you can't build a functional team.

D. You want your co-founder(s) to fit your company culture.

As I said earlier, Jeroen fit our culture. At least he fit what I wanted our culture to be.

Every person you hire either adds or subtracts from your company culture. Therefore, your early hires and founders have a tremendous influence on your company's culture.

Stanford University commissioned a study on the importance of company culture on the success of startups. They found that your chances of success skyrocket, if you have the right culture in place.

It only took me three tries to get the founding team right. Only three (LOL!). Everything fell into place once we got the team, and by definition, the company culture right.

There were other major hurdles along the way. Getting traction certainly was a bigger challenge than I thought it would be.

But, at least in my case, getting the technical co-founder role set was the biggest challenge in getting our company off the ground.

ROUND 3: YOU MAY NOT LIKE IT, BUT YOU NEED A PLAN

Should You Bootstrap or
Take VC Funding?

I f ever there is a question where the answer is "it depends," this is the question.

I've known entrepreneurs who have boot-strapped that have made a fortune. I've also known entrepreneurs who raised VC money that made a fortune. I don't really think the question is whether bootstrapping or VC funding yields you the most amount of money.

The real question is should you bootstrap, or should you take VC funding?

You start by making the "will I make money boot-strapping or with VC funding" the last question you ask.

That's right. Make the amount of money you make bootstrapping or with VC funding the last question you ask.

Instead start with this question:

Will you have a better chance of success bootstrap-ping or with VC funding?

The money will take care of itself, if you take this

approach.

There are many decisions you make when you start a company. However, the most important decision you will make, is who will your investors be.

No matter whether you bootstrap or take VC money, you will have investors.

You want to make sure that you and your investors are aligned from Day One.

If you bootstrap and finance the venture yourself, you had better make sure that your family understands:

- How much money will your company need?

- How will you pay them back?

- When will you pay them back? And...

- Will your investors (your family) continue supporting, you if things don't go according to plan?

If you take VC money, then you need to make sure you and your investors are also aligned.

For example:

- Do you and your investors agree with the long-term vision of the company?

- Do you and your investors agree on how much money your venture is going to need?

- Do you and your investors agree on the key milestones that your venture needs to achieve and when you need to achieve them?

- Do you and your investors agree on what an acceptable outcome for your venture will be?

- Does your venture fit the profile of the fund? In other words, will a successful outcome for your company be a successful outcome for the VC firm?

We haven't even spoken about the emotional concerns you might have:

- Will you be okay losing some control over your company, if you take venture funding?

- Are you willing to take longer to succeed, because of the lack of funding if you bootstrap?

- What if you fail to raise money? The odds are stacked against you (about 100:1 against you) getting venture funding.

Go big or go home?

There are some businesses where you have no

choice but raising venture funding. My company (a semiconductor company) needed to raise large sums of money, so there really wasn't a choice but to pursue venture funding.

There are some businesses where the economics just don't work for venture funding. The majority of new businesses really aren't meant for venture funding.

You may have a choice. The choice really boils down to speed versus control, alignment versus ownership.

How Should You Finance
Your Startup?

One of the investors in my company, Gill, described equity as "fuel" for growth and debt as a "retardant" to growth.

I don't think I agree with Gill. I think the right answer is more about what's right for you and your company.

There is a better way to look at what's right for you. I'll get back to this later. First, let's look at equity and debt.

There are obvious pros and cons to equity and debt:

Equity:

The biggest pro for equity is you don't have any interest to pay and there is no collateral required, but...

The biggest con is that you give up a piece of your company.

Debt:

The biggest pro is that you don't have to give up any equity to get your money, but...

The biggest con is that you have to pay back the interest and the principle.

Whether you give equity or get a loan for your money, you now have to answer to somebody:

It's true that if you get a loan, your lender is not likely to be on your board of directors. However, you will have to give your lender updates on how your company is doing. You'll have to pitch your prospective lenders, just like you'll have to pitch prospective investors.

The better way to look at how to finance your company.

You always have investors, regardless of whether you will self-finance the company, get equity, or get a loan. The key to a successful relationship with the people who finance your company is alignment.

You and your investors need to be in alignment for the goals and outcome for your company.

There are many companies that just don't fit an equity or venture financing model. The question you need to ask is "What are the expectations of my investors?"

Let's go through them one by one:

A. Venture financing.

Professional investors are expecting a multiple on

their money. For early stage VCs, this number is 10X or more.

Let's say you raise $5 million and you give up 30% of your company in return. This means your investors expect at least $50 million on their money.

However, your company has to be worth $167 million for your investors to be happy. The questions you need to ask are:

a. How are you going to make your investors liquid?

In other words, you are either going to need to sell the company or have an IPO. Are these outcomes realistic in your situation, and are these outcomes something you want?

Only pursue VC financing, if the answer is yes.

b. Will a successful exit for your company "move the needle" for the VC fund?

A $50 million exit is a fantastic result for a smallish VC fund of $50 million or $100 million, but it is a yawner for a $1 billion fund because the result will not meaningfully affect the outcome for the fund.

You need to be right sized for the fund you are taking money from. In most cases, VCs will just say no if your company isn't the right size for it. However, you will have problems later, if you somehow get money from a large fund whose expectations are different than yours.

B. Angel financing.

This is pretty similar to venture financing. It covers the $500,000 scenario, since this is probably too small for most venture funds.

The question again comes down to how are you going to make your investors liquid?

Angels probably expect an even higher return than VCs, because they are taking more risk. 30X is a good number to use.

Let's say you give up 20% of your company in exchange for your $500,000. Your investors are expecting a return of $15 million.

That means your company will need to be worth $75 million for them to successfully exit. However, what if you need even more money to get to cash flow positive? Then the numbers go up.

C. Debt.

What do lenders care about? They want to make sure you pay the interest and the principal back.

Remember that banks need collateral for your loan. What is it going to be? If you don't have collateral, then you're likely not going to get a loan.

Finally, you have to work into your financial plan the payback of the interest and the principal. Your runway will be less when you take a loan, so that's the big tradeoff.

Most entrepreneurs underestimate the downside of having a reduced runway! You shouldn't.

Running out of money ahead of schedule kills a lot of companies. Sometimes you can get your bank to work with you to suspend principal payments in times of need.

However, their generosity does not come for free. You'll have to give up something (usually a larger payment later) in return. When you're back is against the wall, your room to negotiate is small.

Some banks will not negotiate with you at all. If you miss a payment, they'll pull the loan. Do your research to see how startup friendly the bank you intend to work with is.

D. Friends, Family and Yourself.

Maybe you can afford to self-fund the company for $500,000. You still have an investor in this case, and you need to be in alignment.

Talk to your spouse or your family and make sure they understand how quickly the loan will be repaid. The oversight when you take money from these sources is less, but they still need to understand when they will get paid back.

How Do You Know It's Time To Hire Your First Employee?

I've been working with "James" for about one year now. James is the CEO of a really cool company. Over the past year, I've had the pleasure of watching James grow his business to a pretty substantial level.

There've been the usual growing pains that any business goes through. You have growth issues, you have contractor issues and you have collection issues, just like any other business.

There's also the constant push and pull between funds available and growth. Managing cash is especially important, when you're bootstrapping like James.

As James prepared to enter into the new year, he developed his plan for the year. One of the smartest things James did, was to create a real financial plan with real metrics that he needed to hit.

We reviewed the plan in November. It was clear, as part of the plan, that James was going to be adding teammates to the team.

The question is when should you pull the trigger

on hiring your first employee?

Every founder goes through the issues James faced. If you bring someone on too early, then you are burning valuable cash. If you bring someone on too late, then you can stunt your growth.

It really is a balancing act.

You've Gotta Have A Plan.

Sometimes you just wing it. You just say, "Hey, we could really use some more help, so I'm just going to hire this person. I know we can't afford it, but I'm going to hire this person anyway."

Six months later, revenue doesn't grow like you hoped it would and you don't have as much money as you expected. Now you're really in a lousy place.

That is why having a financial plan is so important. It's not difficult for you to put together a simple financial plan either.

Let's get started.

You're going to need to gather up everything to do with your company. Let's break this into two parts:

Revenue:

- Your revenue by month
- Your expected revenue by month
- Your current cost of goods (if you are sell-

ing a physical product)

- Your future cost of goods

Your Expenses:

- Salaries for each employee, including yourself

- The expected salaries you're going to pay future employees

- Rent

- Insurance

- Subscriptions

- Office supplies

- Advertising expenses

- Travel expenses

- Anything where you are spending money to run your business

A word of warning.

Many people make the mistake of not truly accounting for all their expenses. I think they do it to give themselves the feeling that things are better than they really are.

You can't make that mistake. You really need to know exactly where you stand. You don't do this, so you can punish yourself. You do this so you know how to responsibly plan when going forward.

Completing this simple exercise puts you ahead of 80% (maybe 90%) of the businesses out there, so congratulations.

Now what?

Put everything in a simple spreadsheet. I recommend using separate tabs for each individual category. You should then have each category feed into a master spreadsheet.

Congratulations. You've just built an income statement for your company. More important, you've built a model for the future growth of your company.

You're now in control of your business. You now know:

- How much cash you're going to need to grow your business, and...

- Exactly where the cash is going, and...

- How many employees you can hire, and...

- When you can hire the employees, and...

- How to have complete visibility of the financial picture of your company.

This is all well and good, but what happens if you don't hit your plan?

Do you want to go a step further? It won't cost you much time.

Great. Let's do it.

One of the smartest things you can do is develop a few different plans:

- A worst-case plan

- A medium-case plan

- A best-case plan

The benefit of having a few different plans, is that you'll be ready to pivot (positively and negatively), depending upon what happens.

Let's say things are going really well. What should you do? You now already have a plan in place that you can use to guide yourself.

Let's say things don't go as well as planned. You also have a plan ready for that case.

The beauty of having these simple plans completed ahead of time, is that you won't have to develop them in a panic. You'll be completely prepared and calm.

The more prepared and calm you are, the more likely you are to make good, rational decisions.

There's one more important thing you need to know about developing financial plans. You will be redoing your financial plan at least every year. As your business grows, resetting your financial plan is the best way to stay in control of your future.

Here's the thing. Growing a business takes cash. Managing your cash (whether you're bootstrapped or venture backed) is a critical discipline on your journey to success.

What if you're way off your financial plan?

Don't worry. It's very normal you to be way off. This is especially true, if you've never done this before.

You'll get better the more times you go through the process. The most important thing is just getting started.

Back to James...

James set his plan in place. He included in his budget the expenses and timing, for hiring new teammates.

The business kept growing and the time came for James to pull the trigger on hiring. James already had recruited his new teammate. In fact, the teammate was already working part-time.

However, expenses were higher than expected in some areas, so there was less cash than expected. What should James do?

By the way, it is normal for expenses to be higher than expected. It happens. However, James could manage the situation from a place of strength, because he had a budget.

James could objectively look at the data and make an objective decision.

James decided to wait a month before bringing on the new teammate full-time. Delaying the new hire would mean James would have to carry the extra load himself. However, it also meant he would be in a strong cash position going forward.

James did one other really smart thing that you should also do. He communicated honestly with his new team member why he was delaying bringing him on.

James' new team member has started, and he is killing it!

Good for James and his new teammate!

Why Paying Yourself A Living Wage Is So Important

You work really hard for years building your company. You're also burning through your savings, as you build your company.

You finally get your company to cash flow positive.

"Thank goodness," you say to yourself. "We're finally free of needing more money.

"The business is now self-sustaining. We can just invest the profits of the business back into the company."

Therefore, it's a rude shock for many entrepreneurs when they realize that their company isn't truly profitable, even though their company is cash flow positive.

How can this be? Cash flow positive means you don't need money anymore, right?

Let me tell you about my friend Mark.

I met Mark a couple of years ago. He has a really cool company that he and his business partner started.

They received some angel funding that helped them

get started, but they are truly bootstrapping.

I love their business and their business model. Their product is unique. Slowly but surely, Mark's company has gained traction.

I tell Mark the same thing every time I see him. "When are you and your partner going start taking a salary?"

Mark's answer is the same each time, "When we're profitable."

I wish I could get Mark to change his mind, but I haven't been successful, yet.

You're only truly profitable, when you and your company are cash flow positive.

Congratulations. Your company is profitable, but you're still draining your bank account.

Guess what? You haven't achieved true profitability yet.

You've achieved true profitability, when you are no longer draining your personal bank account of money.

Somehow, there is a misconception that your investors expect you to starve, while you build your company. Nothing could be further from the truth.

Experienced investors know that it's important for you to make a living wage. In other words, your investors want you to have a big enough salary, so you don't have to worry about paying the bills each month.

I'm not saying that you should pay yourself a huge salary. That doesn't make sense.

However, I am saying that you should, as soon possible, pay yourself enough money, so you can pay your bills.

Why you should pay yourself a living wage.

I recommend to every entrepreneur I work with, that they pay themselves something as soon as possible. Just pay yourself something. Even $100 per month is okay, if that's all you feel comfortable with.

The benefits of paying yourself a small salary go beyond the small amount of money you will make. Let me explain why, except this time I will use a negative example.

There was another entrepreneur I worked with named "James."

James didn't pay himself a salary.

We were going through our bi-weekly review of his company. The revenue was growing, and the company should have been cash flow positive.

In fact, cash from operations was growing, so it didn't make any sense why James' net cash position was dropping.

Then James gave me the answer. "My wife wants me to repay the second mortgage on our home."

"However, there's no loan on the books," I said. "You can't just take money out of the company. You have shareholders."

'You don't understand. We have to pay off that mortgage."

"I understand what you want to do, but you can't do it that way. You're embezzling money from your company."

I instantly knew I would have to stop working with James, because he was embezzling money from his company.

I was bummed.

I had been working with James for a while. James' company had gotten to a nice amount of revenue and was cash flow positive.

James was going to blow it big time, if he didn't change his thought process.

James wouldn't change his mind, so I told James our business relationship was over.

I'm not saying that not paying yourself a salary will result in you doing what James did. Mark is proof of that. However, why put yourself in a bad financial position?

Instead start the discipline of paying yourself a small salary.

- You can start with as small an amount as you want, then...

- Start paying yourself more as the health of your business improves, then...

- Keep increasing the amount you are paying yourself, until you are paying yourself a living wage.

Disciplined cash management leads to better results for your company.

I am a big believer in being what I call being "Appropriately Frugal," when you are the CEO.

Simply put, being appropriately frugal means that you spend money on the important stuff for your business and save money on everything you can save money on.

However, you and your employees are not the area to save money on.

You do want to attract the best employees. You will need to pay them appropriately.

I'm not saying that you should pay your employees crazy salaries. However, I am saying that you should pay your employees market rate. Pay your employees as much as you can, if you can't pay market rate:

- Your employees will feel appreciated, and...

- Your employees will not have to worry about their finances.

The idea that your employees will accept less than market rate because you are just starting, only makes sense if they can afford it. Otherwise, there are three options:

- You will not retain your employees, or...

- You will not hire the best employees, or...

- You will not hire any employees at all.

Why aren't you willing to pay yourself, if you are willing to pay your employees?

Why are you any different than your employees?

You are the most important asset your company has. You will not be at your best, if you are constantly worrying about how you are going to pay your bills each month.

Just remember that true profitability comes when your company AND you are cash flow positive.

Mark, I know you're reading this post. I hope you have decided to pay yourself something.

If you haven't decided to pay yourself something,

then I hope this post helps to change your mind.

What Are the Five Rules You Need To Determine Your Startup Salaries?

"**S**ounds a little rich to me," one of my investors, "Raul," said to me when he asked me what I was going to pay myself as CEO. We had just closed $12 million in Series A funding, and the salary I suggested paying myself was the median for a Series A CEO with that level of funding.

No, it wasn't anywhere near $1 million per year. And no, I didn't adjust my salary because of Raul's protests. The truth is I could have told Raul a ridiculously low number and he would have said that was too high.

There are five basic rules you should follow when you're thinking about salaries for you and your team:

Rule Number 1 For Startup Salaries: You want your funding to last at least 18 months.

The reason why 18 months is the minimum you want your funding to last, is very simple. If your funding only lasts 12 months or less, then you will be in a constant fundraising mode.

Even worse, you might not accomplish enough if your funding dries up too soon to justify more investment. That's why, as a rule of thumb, you want you funding to last at least 18 months to 24 months.

You can do the math and determine what salaries you can afford based on the 18-month rule.

Rule Number 2 For Startup Salaries: You want your salaries to be at the median for any given position.

You've done the math and based on the 18-month rule you have enough funding to pay your team market rate salaries. That's great, and my recommendation is to pay at the median for any given position.

You will end up with a team of mercenaries, if you pay your team at the top end of the salary range. Your team of mercenaries will move on, when a better offer comes in.

You will not be able to recruit the best, if you pay under market when you can afford to pay at the market rate. Your team of B and C players will not be able to execute your plan.

That's why you want to be center cut. You will be able to recruit a great team, if you pay a fair salary, a generous stock option, a great company culture and you give your team exciting work.

Rule Number 3 For Startup Salaries: You want to be proactive about adjusting salaries.

For example, I had two managers, Dave and Shoba. They were doing great work, but they were underpaid. I could have waited and done nothing, but I decided to be proactive and adjust their salaries to where they should have been based on the market.

I wish I could say this was my great invention, but it wasn't. I was following the rules set out in Netflix's culture manifesto. Read it because it is a great blueprint for how to manage your startup.

Rule Number 4 For Startup Salaries: You should never overpay for that one person who will supposedly put you over the top.

Don't think for a second that your team will not find out that you've overpaid this person. People talk, and word will eventually get out.

The rest of you team will resent your overpaid employee. That will make it harder for your overpaid employee to succeed.

Hiring someone at the top end of your salary range will hurt the salary structure for the rest of the team. I've seen this play out. You will likely have a lot of other employees asking for raises above market.

Rule Number 5 For Startup Salaries: Above all, be fair and consistent.

As I said, you have to assume your team is going to talk among themselves about what they are making. You have nothing to fear, if you are fair and consistent in your approach.

However, it's when you are all over the map that you will have problems. Inconsistency builds resentment.

You'll never be perfect. That's why it's important to be proactive and correct any salary mistakes you've made (Rule Number 3). You'll be way ahead of the game, if you start out with a goal of fairness.

ROUND 4: DON'T EXPECT EVERY CO-FOUNDER YOU BRING ON TO WORK OUT

What Are the Warning Signs
Of A Bad Co-founder?

D o you think it's a good idea to propose marriage after your second date?

Good, I didn't think so.

The best analogy for deciding on co-founders is dating. In fact, a co-founder relationship is more intense than a marriage:

- You're working in a very stressful environment for most of your waking hours.

- Money is really tight.

- You don't know if things are going to work out.

The advantage that most married couples have, is the average courtship is 3.3 years in the United States. Nevertheless, the divorce rate is still around 50%.

You are about to enter into an even more intense relationship than a marriage, and you can't wait 3.3 years to find out if your co-founder is going to work out.

Is it any wonder that so many co-founder relation-ships fail?

What can you do to improve the odds that your co-founders are going to work out?

Here are the steps that I would recommend taking. Let's start with:

You shouldn't try to find a co-founder in one or two meetings.

Yes, you will be able to screen some of your candidates out quickly. For example, pass if the candidate isn't excited by the opportunity.

An unexcited co-founder will leave at the first sign of trouble.

Let the relationship move at a natural pace. You'll obviously be able to move faster, if you have a pre-existing relationship with a potential co-founder.

However, it may take several meetings before you and your potential co-founder are comfortable taking the plunge.

What are you looking for?

A. You're looking for fanatics.

Fanatics come in all shapes and sizes. Sometimes fanatics are extroverts. Sometimes they are intro-verts.

Sometimes fanatics have great academic pedigrees, and sometimes they don't.

However, all fanatics are obsessed with your cause.

Fanatics are important to have as co-founders, because fanatics will not give up at the first sign of trouble. They will fight to the death for your cause.

Look for the signs that your potential co-founders are as obsessed with your cause as you are. You'll see it in their excitement about building the company.

B. You're looking for people that have integrity.

You need to walk away from any of your potential co-founders who show any signs that they don't have integrity.

- It doesn't matter how smart they are, and...

- It doesn't matter how great of cultural fit they are, and...

- It doesn't matter how passionate or fanatical they are about the business because...

- You can't work with them if they don't have integrity.

You will end up with a bad result, if you work with a co-founder that lacks integrity.

C. You're looking for people who are really smart in their area(s) of expertise.

Let's say you're looking for an Engineering VP. You want someone who is great at what they do.

It is important that they are not mediocre but great. This is because the level of expertise of the executive has will set the level of expertise of all future hires. Therefore, you have a greater chance of hiring A level engineers, if you start with an A level VP of Engineering.

You have almost no chance of hiring A level engineers, if you start with a B level VP of Engineering.

D. You're looking for people who are cultural fits.

Culture is actually one of the biggest determinants of start-up success, so start thinking about the team you want to assemble before you bring on any co-founders.

I'm not saying that everyone needs to be clones of each other. I am saying that there needs to be a shared set of beliefs that everyone on the founding team agrees on.

Therefore, keep these four things in mind (fanaticism, integrity, smarts and cultural fit) as you are building your relationship with your potential co-founders. Don't be afraid to spend more time or passing, if the relationship isn't moving in the right direction.

The Simple Strategy For Reducing Your Founder Problems

One of the really sad things I've seen as a founder, and now working with other founders, is how often founders don't take their responsibilities as founders seriously.

You are literally putting your career and life in the hands of your fellow co-founders. Your expectation is your co-founders will only join your company, if they are in it for the long haul.

Yet I've seen, time and time again, co-founders betray the trust of their fellow co-founders.

All it takes is for a co-founder not to take this responsibility seriously and your dream is gone. Sadly, this happens all the time.

Over half of the CEOs I work with, are dealing with founder issues. The founder issues vary include:

- The founders are not getting along.

- The founder is not working hard.

- One of the founders is trying to get rid of the CEO.

- Two of the founders are trying to align with each other to force the CEO to make unnecessary changes that will hurt the company.

- One of founders is demanding to be on the board of directors.

I could go on and on.

The point is that founder issues happen much too often.

I had founder issues that almost killed my company. Two of my co-founders stole our IP, left me for dead and then they launched a competing company.

Somehow, I survived, and the company survived, but it took perseverance and a lot of luck.

You don't ever want to get into the position that I was in. The real question is there anything you can do either prevent founder issues before they happen, or, at least, reduce their impact?

I believe there are things you can do to help reduce founder issues. It starts with:

A. You shouldn't drop your standards, when it comes to founders.

It's very tough when you're starting out. Therefore, the temptation is to lower your standards to get a co-founder to join. Let me give you a one-word answer:

Don't.

Don't reach ever.

You will feel good in the moment, when you bring on your mediocre co-founder. However, your happiness will be short-lived. The problems will start immediately, because a founder that can't carry his or her weight will be a burden.

"I need someone, anyone," you'll say.

I know. I've been there too. However, the problem is that when your co-founder's work isn't good, it's often worse than having no co-founder at all.

How well do you think your weak co-founder will be able to recruit?

My bet is not too well.

The old saying that B players recruit C players is true. Now you have the second problem of having more weak people in your company, and...

- Weak people lead to a poor culture, and...

- Weak people lead to a poor execution, and...

- Weak people lead to poor results.

Let's say you've brought on someone you think will be great. Then...

B. You should obey the nine-month rule.

Think of your founder relationships like a marriage, except founder relationships have the added stress of building a company. Is it any wonder that many founder relationships don't work out?

That is why I like the nine-month rule. The nine-month rule is simply a reminder that you should take your time, before you fully commit to working long-term with your co-founder.

I'm not saying you shouldn't work together with your co-founder(s), as if you will work together forever. However, you should put safeguards in place, just in case things don't work out.
For instance, make sure that the equity of you and your co-founder(s) vests over time. Your equity should have at least a four-year vesting period with a one-year cliff.

This means that you can part company with your co-founder without any negative financial consequences, if it is clear that your co-founder isn't going to work out in that first year.

There's nothing sinister or wrong about working this way. One-year vesting cliffs are now pretty standard.

What do you do if you realize you've brought on the wrong co-founder?

C. You need to take action, when things don't work out.

Sometimes you bring on a co-founder that you think will be great and, for whatever the reasons, things don't work out. I had a co-founder that I thought would be great, but he turned out to be a massive disappointment.

The worst thing you can do is doing nothing.

The problem with your co-founder isn't going away. In all likelihood, the problem is just going to get worse.

You are also not the only one who is noticing there's a problem with your co-founder. The rest of your team is very aware of the problems with your co-founder.

However, many people feel like they can't take action against their co-founder. The reality is you have to take action, or your company will suffer or worse.

Most of the time, the action will result in your co-founder leaving the company. That's fine. As I said, over half the people I work with have co-founder issues. All of these cases have resulted in the co-founder leaving the company.

You know what happens when a weak co-founder leaves your company?

Everyone feels better.

It's amazing. You'll likely hear something like this from your team, "What took you so long?"

D. You need to move on.

You'll find that your co-founder really wasn't contributing what you thought and that you can get along just fine without them.

In some cases, you'll find that you don't even have to replace your co-founder. I had a co-founder that wasn't working out, so, after way too long, I fired him.

I immediately starting interviewing replacements for my co-founder. However, I couldn't find anyone I liked. I had his two direct reports working directly for me.

It became obvious that his direct reports were doing the heavy lifting, and he was doing nothing. I decided to promote his direct reports and not replace him.

I've had a few of the CEOs I work with report that they also didn't need to replace a co-founder.

Sometimes not hiring someone, can be the best thing you can do.

Why Your Co-founder Shouldn't Get A Sales Commission

"That sounds like double-dipping," I said to "Al," the CEO of a company I am working with. Al was describing to me his co-founder's idea of getting paid a commission for using his network to refer customers to Al's company.

I asked, "Isn't that what we're paying him for?"

"Yes, it is," Al said. "I feel the same way you do, but I just want to make sure."

Your co-founders shouldn't be worried about making a little extra money on the side.

There are some things that just don't feel right for an early stage startup. Near the top of the list, is a co-founder trying to take extra profits in sales commissions.

Al and I continued our conversation. Al suggested, "What about if I eliminated his equity and we changed him to a consultant?"

"In that case, he wouldn't be a long term fit for company," I responded. "It strikes me that we want co-founders who are fanatical about your mission."

I felt bad for Al. It sucks when you realize that you have a co-founder that's in it for the wrong reason.

You need your co-founders to share your passion for the company.

I'm not saying that your co-founders shouldn't want to make money. They should want to make money.

I am saying that their priority should be the company's success. Lining their pockets with a little extra from sales commissions doesn't line up with the long-term success of your company.

Here are the characteristics that you want from your co-founders:

A. Look for fanatics.

Fanatics come in all shapes and sizes. Sometimes fanatics are extroverts, while other times they are introverts.

Sometimes fanatics have great academic pedigrees, and others don't have those type of credentials.

However, all fanatics are obsessed with your cause.

Fanatics are very important to have as co-founders, because they will not give up at the first sign of trouble. Fanatics will fight to the death for your cause.

Therefore, look for the signs that your potential co-founders are as obsessed with your cause as you are. You'll see it in their excitement about building the company.

B. Look for people that have integrity.

You need to walk away from any of your potential co-founders who show any signs that they don't have integrity.

- It doesn't matter how smart they are, and...

- It doesn't matter how great a cultural fit they are, and...

- It doesn't matter how passionate or fanatical they are about the business because...

- You can't work with them, if they don't have integrity.

You will end up with a bad result, if you work with a co-founder who lacks integrity.

C. Look for people that are very smart in their area(s) of expertise.

Let's say you're looking for an Engineering VP. You want someone who is great at what they do.

This is because the level of expertise of the executive will set the level of expertise of all future hires. You have a greater chance of hiring A level engineers, if you start with an A level VP of Engineering.

You have almost no chance of hiring A level engineers, if you start with a B level VP of Engineering.

D. Look for people who are cultural fits.

Culture is one of the biggest determinants of startup success. Therefore, you should start thinking about the team you want to assemble, before you bring on any co-founders.

I'm not saying that everyone needs to be clones of each other. However, there needs to be a shared set of beliefs that everyone on the founding team agrees on.

Keep these four things in mind (fanaticism, integrity, smarts and cultural fit) as you are building your relationship with your potential co-founders. Don't be afraid to spend more time or passing on the candidate, if the relationship isn't moving in the right direction.

Why Your Technical Co-Founder Can't Be Fired

"**W**hy is Bob with the company?" I asked myself. "He just seems to sit in the corner doing nothing."

Bob was the founder/CEO of the startup I had just joined as VP Marketing. Bob was no longer the CEO, but, for some strange reason, he was still with the company, doing what looked to be nothing.

As I spent more time at the company, I came to realize that Bob had no real responsibilities. It just made no sense to me why was Bob still at the company.

There was one thing that Bob had going for him. He was the technical genius behind the company, and investors are loath to fire the technical genius.

About two months later, Jack, the CEO, was fired by the board. The board hired a new CEO, Dave. However, Bob remained at the company and still without any real responsibilities.

The crazy thing was that the company had a VP Engineering and the company had a CTO. The company didn't need Bob anymore.

Sometimes a founder is kept at a company, because the investors view the founder as a safety net.

Bob was the proverbial security blanket for the investors. If everything went wrong technically, then Bob could pick up the pieces.

The problem was that the company's problems weren't the technology, but the business side of the equation. That was part of the reason why I was brought in.

I started digging into the company's business. The more I dug, the more concerned I got.

The company was doing business with all the major telecom suppliers. That was the good news. The bad news was that Cisco and the other customers were only using the company's product for prototyping, not for production.

It was a house of cards, that was ready to fall. The board came to the same conclusion at the same time that I did, so they fired the CEO.

You have to do the right thing, if your technical co-founder needs to go.

Get your facts straight and present the case to your board of directors that you are GOING to let your technical co-founder go. It's not a question you are asking of your board, it's what you are telling them you are going to do.

Your board is going to push back because your technical co-founder is, well, your technical co-founder. In the board's eyes, you can be replaced. However, it's difficult to replace your technical co-founder.

You need to explain exactly what your plan is going forward. You must tell them factually and unemotionally, why your technical co-founder needs to go.

Sometimes a founder is kept at a company, because the investors are too scared to get rid of the founder.

Years after this experience, I was interviewing to be CEO of another company. Their founder had been pushed out of the CEO role. However, the founder was still at the company.

The company had already cycled through two other CEOs, when I met with them. As I met with the board members, it became clear that the founder was the problem.

Each board member used words like "mercurial" to describe the founder. "He's brilliant, but you're going to need to learn to work with him," they said.

It sounded like a no-win situation to me. This was confirmed after I met him. The founder might be brilliant, but he was also a jerk.

I passed. The company is on CEO number four, and yes, the founder is still there.

ROUND 5: YOU CAN'T GROW YOUR COMPANY IF YOU CAN'T RECRUIT GREAT PEOPLE

How Do You Keep Your Team Highly Motivated?

Y ou want a highly motivated team? You need to walk the walk, and talk the talk every single day.

It's easy to be motivated and enthusiastic when things are going well. The true test of a CEO is how you react when things aren't going well.

For example, you just lost your largest customer. You're still motivated.

Maybe your latest funding round fell through at the worst possible moment. You're still motivated.

You can't ever give in to despair as CEO. Everyone, and I mean everyone, is watching how you deal with adversity. You must stay positive and motivated, regardless of how bad the situation might truly be.

Your team's motivation starts with you and your actions. These actions include:

A. Hiring a great team.

Specifically, you want a team that lives and breathes what your company is working on. You want a team with a great attitude. In short, you want fanatics.

Fanatics keep going, even when times get rough. Fanatics don't care if the odds are against them. Fanatics don't need you to motivate them, because they motivate themselves.

B. Giving your team exciting work to do.

You've got a great team. The easiest way to keep your team motivated, is to give your team exciting work to do.

In fact, you should do more than give your team exciting work. You should give your team more authority, more autonomy and more decision-making ability.

C. You need to be transparent.

You're going to have missteps and mistakes. That's a given.

How you handle the missteps and the mistakes makes all the difference. The natural reaction is to downplay these mistakes.

Don't do that. Use your missteps and mistakes as a way to show your humility.

Your openness and honesty will build trust. Because you have a great team, you'll find that your team will become your partner in helping to solve the problems you encounter building your company.

D. Creating a great work environment – no brilliant jerks.

Do you want to de-motivate your team? Then hire that brilliant jerk you're thinking about hiring.

I've been there. I know that the allure of hiring brilliant jerks is tough to ignore.

You're having trouble finding top talent. I get it. You get a resume. The engineer's background looks promising.

You then interview the engineer. You see that the engineer is technically brilliant, but you can detect that there might be interpersonal issues.

You go ahead and hire the engineer. The complaints start coming.

"We'll make it work," you say to yourself.

One of your best engineers quits and then another.

Don't make the mistake I made. Keep morale high, by keeping the brilliant jerks out of your company.

E. Holding your team accountable.

Great employees want to be held accountable. I'm not suggesting that you micromanage your team. I am actually a big believer in giving your team as much autonomy as possible.

I am suggesting you set goals and objectives for your team and hold them (and you) accountable for meeting the goals.

F. Use Kaizen, the theory of small incremental goals.

Since we're on the subject of goals, use Kaizen to build momentum in your organization. Kaizen is the concept of using small, incremental goals to achieve larger goals.

I'm not saying you shouldn't set your big, hairy audacious goal. I am saying that setting small, achievable incremental goals is the way to get to your big goal.

For example, let's say you have a long-term goal of $10 million/year in revenue. You should absolutely set that as a long-term goal.

You should also set your monthly goals accordingly. If your first month's revenue goal is $1,000, then set your first monthly goal at $1,000.

Make sure that you hit the goal!

You do it again the next month, by setting your revenue goal at $1,500. You then keep meeting your short-term goals every month.

This is how you build momentum. It is also how you keep your team motivated on the road to your long-term big hairy audacious goal.

G. Setting rewards for hitting your goals – celebrate your successes.

Building a company should be fun for you and your team. There is a lot of grinding you have to do. However, there's no reason you can't celebrate your success along the way.

Give your team a reward when you hit certain objectives. For example, you just launched your first product, on schedule no less, so you give your team free movie tickets.

You had your first month of $1,000 in revenue (remember the goals are small at the start), so you give each member of your team a $10 Starbucks gift card, when you hit the goal.

You just got to cash flow positive (this is a huge goal for any startup). You give every member of your team a $1,000 bonus and throw a blowout party that, momentarily, sets you in the red.

You get the idea. Make the goals and the rewards consistent with the current stage of your company.

It is important to make the rewards frequent, such as at least once every quarter. That way you keep the dopamine coming.

H. Getting rid of the bad apples.

I already told you to stay away from brilliant jerks. However, what should you do about the employees that aren't working out, even if they are a founder?

Everyone's watching what you're going to do, when someone isn't working out. The longer you wait to take action, the worse things will get.

Your team will lose its motivation, if there are disruptive employees or those that are just not performing well. You have no choice, if you want a motivated team. You need to take action and remove the underperforming employees.

The reaction from your team when you do take action is always the same. "What took you so long?"

Your employees always know who needs to go, long before you do.

As you can see, there are many things you can do to keep your team motivated. You can hire a great team, give your team exciting work, be transparent, create a great work environment, hold your team accountable, use Kaizen, set rewards for hitting your goals and get rid of your bad apples.

Remember, most importantly, your team's motivation starts with you and your actions.

What Are The Six Rules For Building Loyal Teams?

"**I**t was my fault. I screwed up," I told the CEO. "You should be screaming at me, not him!"

I didn't want Steve (my boss) to take the beating for my screw-up. I wanted the CEO to tear into me, not Steve.

The CEO didn't care. He kept his guns pointed at Steve and he wouldn't relent.

Ten minutes later, it was over. Steve was bloodied from the bullets he had taken. The CEO had made his point and left the meeting.

I was indebted to my boss forever. You are fortunate in your career to have one or two really good bosses or mentors, and Steve was one of the good ones.

Each mentor provides you with different knowledge. I only worked for Steve for about one year before he retired, but he had a lasting impact on me.

Steve had, in many ways, the toughest job in the company. Imagine being in the middle of a battle with bullets flying in every direction at you and you get the general idea.

However, Steve always carried himself with class and grace. He was a beacon of calm in a very stormy ocean.

Steve's people were also incredibly loyal to Steve.

Why is loyalty so important?

You could start by asking Julius Caesar about Brutus. I think Shakespeare has already covered that one.

- Betrayal brings down governments, and...

- Betrayal can destroy or nearly destroy companies, and...

- Betrayal can destroy teams.

On the flipside, a loyal team full of A players can do just about anything it sets it mind to. That's why it's so important to create an environment that creates loyalty.

Loyalty starts with you, the CEO.

I think you have it completely backwards, if you just expect people to be loyal. It is true that is what should happen in an ideal world.

However, you must create an environment that allows the best chance for loyalty. Great leaders naturally understand this.

The first rule of building loyal teams: have the backs of your teammates.

When your team knows you have their backs, they will go to the end of the Earth for you. Every one of Steve's reports (not just me) felt tremendous loyalty to Steve.

They demonstrated their loyalty through hard work and going the extra mile.

The second rule of building loyal teams: you should never ever, ever scrimp on integrity.

This should probably be rule number one but having the backs of your teammates fit better in the flow of the story.

What's the most important attribute that any employee can have?

Is it being smart? No.

Is it being passionate? No.

Is it fit within the company? No.

It's integrity without a doubt. Integrity is about having strong moral principles. In other words, integrity is the key ingredient in finding loyal employees.

You know the genius you want to hire with a little bit of questionable character?

Don't.

That's right. Just don't hire him.

Every time. Every single time I have made the mistake of hiring a really smart person whose integrity was in question, I have lived to regret it.

Every. Single. Time.

The third rule for building loyal teams: You should always promote from within, whenever possible.

I am always looking for ambitious people to bring onto the team. Ambitious people want to grow and be promoted.

I am not saying to promote people, just to keep them happy. What I am saying is that rewarding excellent work with a promotion is always the way to go.

Back to my story of working with Steve...

The company was growing at a rapid rate, so management was always looking for people to take on more responsibility. Steve was retiring (a massive loss for the company). One of the last things he did, was request that the CEO promote me.

I knew Steve's track record of promoting his people. I knew I was likely to be rewarded for my work. Sure enough, that held true.

The fourth rule of building loyal teams: give your

team the freedom to create.

The natural tendency of all companies as they grow, is to create more rules and procedures. RESIST IT AT ALL COSTS! You should instead make the bold decision to increase employee freedom.

We did, and it paid off for the team. Do it, and your team's motivation will go way up. A more motivated team is a loyal team.

The fifth rule of building loyal teams: sometimes you get it wrong and you need to fix things.

You can do everything right as a manager and still get it wrong. There's always going to be someone who doesn't work out.

You need to let the person go, whether the reason is poor performance or disloyalty. Loyalty to the team involves removing people who are not performing.

The sixth rule of building loyal teams: you need go beyond the rules to do what's right.

There are good rules and there are rules that are made to be broken. A great leader knows when to break the rules to build loyalty.

There are two CEO's I worked for who stand out: one for the right reasons and the other for the wrong reasons. I'll start with the right way to do things.

That same CEO that tore my boss Steve apart, also

had a heart of gold. He made his personal physician (who was on the board of Stanford Hospital) available to his management team.

I had a serious family medical issue, and I needed a second opinion. The next thing I knew, I was getting a second opinion from the CEO's physician. That's the right way to do things.

You'd better believe that built loyalty.

The following is the wrong approach.

I worked for a CEO who was very old school. He made employees take vacation time for any doctor visits taken during normal business hours.

The rule was silly, stupid and illegal in California. It pissed off employees, because it felt like school, where you needed a hall pass to go to the bathroom. It also felt that the CEO was being cheap at the employees' expense.

Interestingly enough, the CEO ended up paying for his foolishness with his job. Even more interesting is how he lost his job.

That's right. He was betrayed by his own employees.

How Do You Build A Great Team?

"**B**rett, you look like you're a million miles away," "Randy" said to me.

Randy was right. I wasn't focused at all on him. I was waiting for Tina to come into my office.

"Where's Tina?" I asked.

You see, this wasn't a normal meeting. It was a meeting to terminate Randy. Tina was supposed to be there to witness the termination.

We had set up an employee meeting with our benefits provider, so Randy could leave without feeling humiliated. Tina was introducing our benefits provider to the employees, and I had to wait.

"Tina!"

Finally, Tina came into my office.

My heart rate shot way up. Then I let Randy know we were terminating his employment.

I ended my comments with, "I'm sorry."

Randy said, "I'm sorry too."

Tina ushered Randy into her office.

I felt sad. Really, really sad.

I just let a really talented person go.

Why? Randy was, to put it mildly, a handful to work with. There were too many complaints from too many people.

Too many people were quietly miserable. They weren't complaining, but you could see the frustration written on their faces.

You have to do the right thing as the CEO.

I had a choice to make: Keep a very talented senior member of the team and let everyone in the company just deal with him, or I could terminate him.

I choose to terminate Randy because I felt, as talented as he was, the interpersonal problems would hurt the company, if I just let things stay the same.

The reality is that Randy didn't fit with the team and the culture we were building.

One of the most overlooked areas of running a successful business or managing a team is the culture.

When everything is going great, culture doesn't matter. Look out below when things are going bad. That's when company culture matters.

And believe me, every company goes through bad times.

Your survival and your company's survival might depend upon the team you have built.

Let me give you another example.

My company was going through a very difficult time raising money. We had a term sheet, but our investors wanted another new investor (in addition to the one we had) to join the syndicate.

We had four prospective new investors. However, we were still four weeks or so away from getting a commitment from one of the new investors.

We had a board meeting and our investors decided to shut the company down.

Their decision took me by surprise. I suggested to the board that we put the employees on minimum wage for the next six weeks, so we could get a commitment from at least one of the four potential investors.

The board agreed.

The tough part was telling the employees. I didn't know how they would react.

Would they get mad?

Would they quit en masse?

I didn't know what would happen.

We had a company meeting the day after the board meeting like we always did.

I told the employees we had no choice but going to minimum wage to save the company.
I answered questions until there were no more questions to be answered. I thanked the employees for their support at the end of the meeting.

I still didn't know what type of response the employees would have.

As the meeting ended, they responded. The employees applauded – all of them.

I was floored. I have never been so proud of a group of people, as I was that day.

However, I was still worried about losing our best employees.

We didn't lose a single one, and three of the four investors eventually committed to investing.

I believe the reason the employees didn't quit was in large part due to the quality of the people we hired.

What do you do?

How do you create a cohesive company culture?

Should you hire the genius jerk that might save the

company?

It starts with the people you hire.

The leader sets the culture for the company, division, or group. There's an old saying: the fish stinks from the head down. Simply put, a bad leader sets a bad culture, and a good leader sets a good culture.

A leader can have whatever culture he or she wants in mind. However, it is the people the leader surrounds herself or himself with that determines the culture.

In other words, you cannot just decree a culture. You hire (and fire) a culture.

What should you look for in the people you hire, and what should you look for in the team you are about to join?

Here are the four things I always look for:

A. Integrity.

Need we go any further? Why would you ever hire someone, if they don't have integrity? Actually, I think we do need to go a little further.

Everyone – everyone – is occasionally faced with the dilemma that arises when you're interviewing a clearly talented individual who seems a bit ethically iffy. Don't hire them. Ever. No amount of ability makes up for a lack of integrity.

B. Smart.

We want people who are very smart. Who doesn't, right? It is surprising how often I see people who only hire those who clearly aren't as smart as they are.

Don't be intimidated by those who might have something you don't. Be grateful that you can add them to your team.

C. Passion.

I don't care how much intelligence and integrity an employee has. They will not work out, if they are not passionate about what they do. They also won't work out, if they're not passionate about what you do.

When I interview someone, I always look for people who are committed enough to my cause to have done their research and found out as much as possible about my company.

D. Company fit.

People frequently overlook the importance of cultural fit. Desiring cultural fit does not mean that we want people who are clones of each other.

Diversity is vital. However, diverse employees better mesh well with each other. Throw a bunch of diverse ingredients that don't go together into a pot, and you have a horrible meal. Throw the right stuff into that pot, and you've got gourmet cuisine. Aim for a five-star group of employees.

What if you inherit a team?

Let's start with what to do if you are the leader: get the right people on the bus, and the wrong people off the bus. You should then figure out what seats the right people should be in on the bus.

Evaluate everyone based on the simple four-part criteria above:

Do They Have Integrity?

Are They Smart?

Do They Have Passion?

Do They Fit the Company Culture?

One big word of caution:

Don't rush to judgment!

Remember that when you're interviewing, every candidate is trying to impress you, so everyone (except for the truly negative) will be on their best behavior. The great employees to build around, may not reveal themselves for a long time.

Consistency is the key.

Years ago, I took over the division a company that was in need of a complete overhaul. Many of the initial team I inherited worked hard during the initial transition period.

It was only several months into the turnaround that the great teammates became clear:

- Great teammates do great work, day in and day out for the long haul, and...

- Great teammates always have integrity, and...

- Great teammates always work smart, and...

- Great teammates always have passion, and...

- Great teammates always fit in the company culture.

Once in their career, everyone should experience what it is like to work with a great team. You will never accept working in any other environment once you do.

How Do You Stop Employees from Going To Your Competitors?

I was recently asked the question, "What should I do to keep an employee who has quit, from leaving."

I was happy to answer the question, because I have a perfect batting average as CEO of keeping employees from quitting.

That's right. 0.00%.

Employees, in my experience, have usually made up their mind when they resign. It's become an emotional issue, and it's very difficult to overcome emotion. This accounts for my perfect batting average.

My view is simply, "Don't let employees get to the point, where they want to quit."

If you treat people well, have a great culture and give people exciting work, then employee retention goes way, way up. Here's how we did it at my company:

We unabashedly stole our company culture from

Netflix with a little bit of Zappos and Sandy Koufax thrown in.

We were thieves and robbers, but I'd like to think we were just being smart.

I've always felt you can take inspiration from many different sources, not just from your industry.

I was fortunate to be exposed to Reed Hastings' (CEO of Netflix) wonderful culture manifesto, right after we started operations. Many parts of it resonated with me. I shared it with our executive staff, and they also liked it.

How do Zappos and Hall of Fame Baseball Pitcher Sandy Koufax fit in? We'll get there. For now, let's focus on the six things we stole, er, borrowed from Netflix.

I want to emphasize again that I think Netflix's culture is fantastic. However, these six things really stood out to us:

A. Adequate performance gets a generous severance package.

Nothing kills a company quicker than mediocre coworkers. This is especially true at a start-up, where there is tremendous pressure to hire key personnel. Think about a 20-person start-up with one bad employee.

That translates to 5% of your workforce being ineffective. As a result, one person can really wreak havoc. Hiring mistakes will happen, and you need to take quick action. That being said, handle these terminations with class and grace.

B. Brilliant jerks.

Diverse styles are fine, as long as the person embodies the company values. It's easy to tolerate jerks when things are going well, but things don't always go well. One jerk, especially in a small startup, can destroy a company.

Hiring pressure can push you to hire a jerk, and you will likely regret it. We did hire a couple of jerks along the way. Shortly thereafter, they were given a generous severance package.

C. Responsible people thrive on freedom and are worthy of freedom.

The natural tendency of all companies as they grow, is to create more rules and procedures. RESIST IT AT ALL COSTS!

Instead, make the bold decision that Netflix made to increase employee freedom. We did, and it paid off for the team. Do it, and your team's motivation will go way up.

D. There is no vacation policy, or said another way, take as much vacation as you want as long as long you get your work done.

You're worried about abuse, of course, and you're right. There will be abuse, if you haven't hired the right people.

Hire the right people and this policy is self-correcting. By the way, a hidden benefit is that you don't have to financially reserve for vacation when you go to a no vacation policy.

E. Act in the company's best interest.

The executive staff had a vigorous debate about enacting a rigid expense and travel policy. Again, the worry was abuse.

Our theory was that it's self-correcting. Employees that continually abused the policy would be given a generous severance package.

I do remember one of my co-founders who tried to expense a one-mile car trip to interview a candidate. Can you imagine receiving a $0.55 expense report? I couldn't. We talked about it in our staff meeting, and one of his peers set him straight.

F. No fixed (raise pool) budgets.

You have to look at what the market is for a particular role every year. For example, if the salaries for senior design engineers go up 15% in a year, we would increase the pay of senior design engineers commensurate with the market.

We quickly gained a reputation for fairness by

working this way. Employees knew we rectified any pay inequities, and it helped build employee loyalty and employee retention.

Okay, so you want to know how Zappos and Sandy Koufax fit in. Here we go.

Let's start with Zappos, the online shoe retailer that Amazon bought. I was flying, I think, to Chicago, when I read an article in American Way magazine article about Zappos CEO Tony Hsieh. That led me to buy his book, "Delivering Happiness."

We loved Zappos' customer service model of no scripts and letting the customer service team make the decisions. We, therefore, modeled our customer service organization after Zappos'. We regularly received accolades from our customers about our tremendous customer service.

We embraced Sandy Koufax's "Keep it Simple" mantra. Koufax was a two-pitch, and on many days only a one-pitch, starting baseball pitcher for the Los Angeles Dodgers. Most starting pitchers throw at least four pitches. Koufax dominated baseball by honing just two.

It worked brilliantly in baseball, and simplicity in business is a key to success. Take notice whenever you hear someone say, or, better yet, you hear yourself say, "It's complicated." It usually isn't that complicated.

All of this is great, but there is one more thing you,

as a leader, need to do, no you MUST DO, to retain employees:

You need to really care about your team.

Here are a couple of examples of how to do it right and how to do it wrong:

How to do it right: My Mom was diagnosed with cancer, when I was working for Maxim Integrated Products. Maxim's CEO, the late Jack Gifford, made his personal physician, who I believe was a board member at Stanford Hospital, available to consult with. You bet that built loyalty.

How to do it wrong: I was working at another company as a senior executive, when my daughter was born. I took a little time off to be with my wife and daughter.

The CEO of this company was pissed that I took even one day off, and he made it known. Not just to me, but to all the other senior executives. I left the company within a year.

By the way, my Mom is still going strong 24 years later.

I love you Mom.

How Do You Handle Ethics
Issues When You're CEO?

I was walking around the office late one Friday afternoon. I was chatting with everyone, cubicle by cubicle, about was going on. Then I got to "Chris's'" cubicle, and I noticed something on his computer screen.

Chris was looking at porn.

Chris quickly switched from the porn website to another website. I went back to my office, and I thought about what I should do.

It was instantly obvious.

I called Chris, and asked him to come to my office. One minute later, Chris was in my office.

"Close the door," I said.

Then I continued. In a very calm voice, I said, "I noticed what you had on your computer, and we just can't have that here.

"If it happens again, we will have no choice but to let you go. Do you understand?"

Chris said, "I do understand."

"Okay, then get back to work."

You can choose to ignore the small ethical challenges, or you can do the right thing.

It would have been so easy just to ignore what Chris was doing. It was just porn. Boys will be boys, right?

Looking at porn on your computer at work may not sound like a big deal, but it is a big deal.

Your culture isn't something you can just turn on and off.

Who knows who in the company would have been offended because of what Chris was doing?

You can bet that wasn't the first time Chris had surfed the web at work looking at porn. This was just the first time Chris was caught.

He knew I saw him. If I did nothing, then Chris would have felt comfortable doing it again.

You have a responsibility to keep your workplace a place everyone feels comfortable in. The second you look the other way, is when your culture suffers forever.

Your culture is your most important asset.

You may be surprised to hear this, but your company culture is the best indicator of whether your company is going to be successful. Therefore, you want to protect your company culture at all costs.

That's why you can't ever look the other way when you know something is wrong. You are the CEO. If you're ethically challenged, how can you expect anyone else not to be ethically challenged?

Why Your Company Culture
Is the Key To Your
Company's Success

A good friend of mine just a joined a hot startup here in the Silicon Valley. The company is on fire.

The executive team has previously been uber-successful. Revenue is getting near what I call escape velocity. They've exceeded their revenue goals every quarter for two straight years.

I think my friend is going to hit it big.

However, lately when I see him, he's been complaining. Things seem to be changing at his new company, and not for the better. When I ask him what's wrong, he says it has to do with a new executive the company has hired.

The importance of culture on your company's success.

My friend's company just hired a new VP, and this new VP is creating havoc. My friend is telling me that the new VP is not meshing well with his new team.

According to my friend, the new VP is rude and obnoxious. He appears not to be building confidence with his new team. The new executive is not shy either. He is displaying his bad temper in front of the CEO and other senior executives.

Isn't it amazing how hiring just one person (especially a senior executive) can totally change the dynamics of a company?

My friend is quietly going crazy, because this new VP is making life miserable for him and others. I keep reassuring my friend that eventually, the CEO will get to his enough point and fire the VP. My only two questions are:

How long will it be before the new VP leaves the company?

How much harm will the new VP cause before he leaves?

That's why culture is critical to your company's success.

The realization that culture is critical to your company's success is nothing new. All the way back in 2002 (ancient times, I know...), James Baron and Michael Hannan published the results of the eight-year study of startup cultures called, "Organizational Blueprints for Success in High-Tech Start-Ups: Lessons from the Stanford Project on Emerging Companies".

The authors studied over 200 startups. The results of their study indicate that a startup's culture has a massive impact on the probability of success. In fact, the culture choice of the company's founders likely has the most impact on a company's chances of success. There are five types of culture that are prevalent in startups. They are[1]:

Star: "We recruit only top talent, pay them top wages and give them the resources and autonomy they need to do their job."

Commitment: "I wanted to build the kind of company where people would only leave when they retire."

Bureaucracy: "We make sure things are documented, have job descriptions for people, project descriptions and pretty rigorous project management techniques."

Engineering: "We were very committed. It was a skunk-works mentality and the binding energy was very high."

Autocracy: "You work, you get paid."

Do you want to get your company to some sort of liquidity event, such as an IPO or a sale? Then, the Commitment culture is your best chance of success:

I also know from personal experience that culture

is crucial to a company's success. In fact, the culture was great at successful companies I worked at.

However, is culture really the most important thing? I would have thought money, followed by idea and culture, so I found that information to be mind-blowing.

There is no denying the information. There is an unbelievable correlation between culture and success.

Why don't founders think about culture first?

I can only go by own personal experience. The money (or at least the promise of money) came first. I was asked by a venture capital firm to incubate a company as an Entrepreneur in Residence (EIR), so I thought the money was in the bag.

The money wasn't in the bag. Surprise.

I started my company with two co-founders: Jim and John (not their real names). I was the CEO, Jim was the marketing guy and John was the engineering guy.

I knew all the steps that were necessary and I knew exactly how to implement them. However, we got tripped up, long before we could implement the plan.

We didn't mesh as a team.

John didn't understand my value. He convinced Jim

they didn't need me. They quit the company, and started another company built on my idea and plan.

I am sure that Jim and John thought they left me for dead. I am sure they thought I would just give up, go home and move on with my life.

I didn't move on with my life.

I recruited other co-founders, and we started raising money. Jim and John started raising money as well.

We were successful in raising funding and they weren't. I would bet that a lot of companies never get off the ground because of founder mismatch. Therefore, you can already see that culture, even in its most basic form, is critical to your success.

Culture is critical. Throughout the life of your company, culture will be a determinant of your success and failure. Every employee you hire, and (more importantly) every employee you don't hire is critical to your success.

Every employee or co-founder you bring on has a major impact on your culture. Think about it. Let's say you have four co-founders, and you are going to add a fifth. That new co-founder will increase your workforce by 20%!

That's a huge number. Every new hire you make is critical. That is why you also need to let go of anyone who doesn't work out. Their impact on your culture will be huge.

However, as important as the employees are to your company culture (and they are very important), you, the CEO, are the most important influence on your company's culture.

Another example from my past:

I certainly want to hire superstars, because there's no doubt that superstars can produce great results. However, not all superstars work well as a team. Not all superstars are loyal.

I'll never forget years ago, when I was working at Maxim Integrated Products. The CEO, the late Jack Gifford, liked hiring smart young people. These people weren't superstars yet, but they might become superstars later.

Jack wasn't afraid to hire brash, outspoken people. He always felt people would get along.

One day I was put on the interview list for someone who had just received his MBA from the University of Chicago, one of the best schools in the country. Apparently, this fellow had written a letter to Jack, so Jack decided to interview him.

The guy was brilliant, and he certainly had looked like he could be a superstar. However, he also was a grade A asshole. I wanted nothing to do with this person.

However, hiring him was Jack's decision, not mine. Jack wanted to hire him, so the company made him an offer. I held my breath.

Thank goodness the offer wasn't accepted. It's sometimes better to be lucky than good. I knew we/ I just got very lucky.

Why? We had a great culture, where people worked hard and collaborated. They believed in the company, and they were committed to the company's future.

When there was a threat to the company, everyone would rally together. This person from the University of Chicago was clearly not a good fit in our culture.

At some point, you will not know when, you and your company are going to be shaken to the core.

What will your superstar team do?

Are they going to support you?

Are they going put in the extra effort necessary?

Are they going to walk?

Your team's belief in the company, and more importantly, their loyalty to the company will be huge determining factor.

Do you really, really want your startup to win?

The most important part of building your startup is not:

- The market you choose, or...

- The product(s) you sell, or...

- The amount of money you raise

It's the company culture!

Great leaders are always learning how to do things better.

Let's say you realize your culture is more in line with an autocratic culture. Can you change your culture to a more committed culture?

Of course, you can, but it will not be easy.

You, the CEO, are going to have to change.

You can't just decree a new culture. It doesn't work that way. You truly have to embrace and believe in what you're doing.

You're going to have to change first. I mean truly change. You're then going to have to overcome the doubt your team has.

It will take time and a consistent effort to get there, but even a slight change is worth it.

Can you do it?

The success of your company depends on it.

1. From: Organizational Blueprints for Success in High-Tech Start-Ups: Lessons from the Stanford Project on Emerging Companies by James Baron and Michael Hannan

What's Your EQ And
Why Does It Matter?

"You have an EQ of zero!" Ken yelled at me.

"What the hell is an EQ?" I asked.

"Perfect!" Ken screamed back. He then hung up the phone. Those were the last words Ken ever said to me.

Just like that, a twenty-year friendship and business relationship ended forever.

Ken was a co-founder of my company. More importantly, I considered him to be a close friend.

I had lunch with Ken the day before, for our weekly 1:1. I pushed him pretty hard at lunch, because he wasn't performing well.

I looked down at Ken's feet and he wasn't wearing socks.

It triggered a memory of when we were raising money. We were in a diligence meeting with a VC. I vividly remembered the VC looking disapprovingly at Ken's sockless feet.

I told Ken that day with the VC, he needed to wear socks.

At lunch, I said nothing. However, I was a little pissed off.

Over lunch, I went over each of my concerns with Ken. He listened without saying a word.

I ended our lunch conversation by saying, "Make life easier for us."

Ken didn't say a word, as we drove back to the office.

The next morning at 9 AM, I received an email from Ken. The title was "Resignation:"

"Brett,

I've decided to make your life easier by resigning. I will no longer come into the office. However, I will make my last day May 30th, so I can vest one more month of stock."

I immediately got on the phone and called Ken. That's when Ken yelled at me, "You have an EQ of zero!"

I did some deep thinking when the call ended. I then called the board of directors to let them know that Ken resigned. The first thing I did was Google "EQ". Here's what I found on psychcentral.com:

"For most people, emotional intelligence (EQ) is more important than one's intelligence (IQ) in attaining success in their lives and careers. As individuals, our success and the success of the profession today depend on our ability to read other people's signals and react appropriately to them."

I asked myself a lot of questions:

"Should I have pushed Ken?"

"Was I out of line?"

"What did I miss?"

The reality is that I wasn't being honest with myself or with Ken. I think we had both known for months things weren't working well.

I was hoping that he would suddenly get motivated and start working the way he used to work years ago.

It wasn't going to happen.

The way I should have handled my conversation with Ken, was just stating the specific facts about his performance. I should then have asked him a question, not with anger, but with empathy:

"We know there's a lot of hard work and personal sacrifice needed in your role. I am just wondering whether you really want to do this anymore?"

Maybe we would still be friends, if I handled the situation in this way. I don't know.

I did know that was I was bummed out for two

reasons:

1. A dear friend was no longer a friend.

2. I thought my EQ (after I learned what it was) was pretty high. It wasn't. I would have sensed the personal issues Ken was dealing with, if my EQ was higher.

The reality is you can always get better, no matter how good you think you are.

Growing your EQ requires five things:

A. Self-Awareness.

You have to be able to recognize your emotions and the effects your emotions have on others. You also need to be self-confident.

B. Self-Regulation.

How well do you control your emotions?

C. Motivation.

You need to set clear goals and have a positive attitude.

D. Empathy.

You need to have the capacity to understand or feel what another person is experiencing from within the other person's frame of reference.

E. Social Skills.

You need to be able to understand, empathize and communicate well with others to have a high EQ.

Effective communication is everything in the working world. It doesn't matter if you are a manager, a CEO or an employee.

Think about everything and everyone you have to effectively communicate with:

- Employees
- Board of directors
- Investors
- Peers
- Customers
- Vendors
- Trade press

The list goes on and on.

OK, so how do you become an effective communicator?

This is what is effective for me with my personality:

A. You should be direct and to the point.

I like to tell it like it is. I don't oversell, and I don't undersell.

I prefer to stick with the facts. Employees want to know where they stand, so I work hard to win points by being honest.

B. You should under promise and overdeliver.

It is very important to set realistic expectations, especially with your board and investors. I will give you an example of how not to do it.

We provided engineering updates every board meeting, when the company started. The schedules we used were "perfect" schedules.

In other words, we looked bad every time we had a slip. We looked bad in the board's eyes, even though our execution was good.

We changed our scheduling technique using the "critical chain" methodology. This actually improved our engineering performance and our standing with the board.

C. You should be transparent.

Share as much as possible with your team. Yes, there will be leaks, but it is worth it.

Treat your team like adults, and the team will respond positively, even to bad news.

In fact, they may have ideas of how to solve the problem. You will earn the team's loyalty and support working this way.

D. You should be positive in voice and body language.

Every movement, speech, email and everything else you do, is analyzed by your team.

Hell can be breaking out around you, but you need to have a steady hand at the wheel. Your team is going to take their lead from you.

E. You should fill in the blanks.

You always need to tell the team what you mean, and what you don't mean. Telling people what you don't mean is critical, because your team will fill in the blanks for you -- and you may not like what the team fills in.

That's all well and good, but improving your EQ revolves around your empathy.

Truly caring for the people you work with, is the most important skill you will need to succeed in business and life.

We all have heard the story of the heartless person who clawed his way to the top over a pile of dead bodies.

That's one way to succeed. You succeed (if you succeed at all) at a horrible price to yourself and those around you.

There is another way to success. It is through empathy and high standards.

I am not saying that you should roll over. In fact, I'm saying just the opposite.

What I am saying is you can truly care for the people you work with and hold them accountable. But:

You can't fake caring. You will fail spectacularly, if you try and fake caring.

You need to really get to know the people you work with. This includes not only them, but also their spouses and children.

You will need to hold the people you work with to an even higher standard. Yes, an even higher standard. This applies not just to the physical results they produce, but with the way they contribute to the organization.

Do you truly want to be the best?

Then you will need to deal with the not just the good stuff, but the not-so-good stuff:

- Death

- Cancer

- Addiction

- Depression

- Aging parents

It's a long list, with many other life issues that we all face.

You will need large doses of empathy to help your team through these life issues. You will also need creative solutions. For example:

What if you have an employee that is diagnosed with cancer?

Will you:

Give the employee two weeks of sick pay and then tell the employee she is on her own?

Say the hell with the company's sick pay policy and decide that the employee is on paid indefinite leave, until she is well enough to return?

The empathetic leader puts the employee on paid indefinite leave, because it's the right thing to do. Yes, it costs more, but that's what you are supposed to do.

Guess what? It feels really good to help people.

In fact, you really regret when you are unsuccessful (Ken being a prime example). That drives you to always do the right thing. It may seem more costly (emotionally and financially), but it is actually far easier.

What Traits Do Your Worst Employees Share?

"**Y**ou need to meet your revenue numbers," I said to our VP Sales, "Tommy." Tommy had been on the job for about one month and already things were going sideways.

"Well, okay," Tommy meekly responded.

That's not exactly the awe-inspiring response you want from your sales lead. Tommy didn't seem to care. It was as if he expected to fail.

In fact, I already knew that Tommy wasn't going to succeed as our VP Sales. I couldn't stand Tommy. His attitude just sucked.

A bad attitude is at the top of my list of traits of the bad employees I've hired over the years. Here are the other common traits of the bad employees I've hired. You can almost be guaranteed that your bad hires will have at least one of these qualities:

A. Your worst hires will lack integrity.

"I was speaking to someone at the gym who works at Maxim (or biggest competitor), and she already knew that you put everyone on minimum wage,"

Tommy said to me the Monday after we had put the staff on minimum wage the previous Friday.

Moving the team to minimum wage for six weeks was a necessary step to keep the company alive. If we didn't take this step, our investors would have shut the company down.

Tommy was out Friday, so I told him over the weekend about our intentions. Tommy said, "That (the salary he would be getting when we moved to minimum wage) won't even cover the cost of gas."

"You're going to lose a lot of people," Tommy said. I didn't say a word in response, but I knew that Tommy was lying.

I suspected that what really happened, was that Tommy was upset that he was making minimum wage, so he told this person at the gym what happened. Now he was covering his tracks.

When you can't trust someone anymore, then, no matter how brilliant the person might be, it becomes difficult to work with them. Tommy had other problems including:

B. Your worst hires will not be passionate.

You could certainly cite Tommy's unenthusiastic response to me saying you have to meet your numbers, as proof that Tommy wasn't passionate about his job. However, the problems started the first week Tommy started with us.

We had a sales review meeting that I used to run. The meeting was at 4 PM, and I had told Tommy about the meeting.

The sales team walked into the conference room at 4 PM, but there was no Tommy. I asked the team, "Where's Tommy?"

The team said they hadn't seen him. I called Tommy on his mobile. "Tommy, we're having the sales review meeting right now. Where are you?"

"I'm on my way home. Go ahead and have the meeting without me."

Huh?

Needless to say, I was a little surprised by Tommy's response. I know that if I was in his shoes, there's no way I would have missed that meeting.

Tommy, on the other hand, didn't seem to think it was a big deal. But there were more problems with Tommy.

C. Your worst hires will not fit with the company culture.

I knew that Tommy didn't seem to fit our culture before I hired him. Yet I still hired him. That just goes to show that you should never lower your hiring standards for anyone, no matter how good you think they are.

My worries about Tommy fitting in were proven to be correct. Tommy was, what you might call, "a behind closed doors" person in an open-door culture.

Tommy always seemed to be in an office or a conference room talking to someone with the door shut. We had an inclusive positive culture, but all it takes is one person with a bad attitude to bring everyone else down.

One of the biggest residual issues you have with someone that doesn't fit your culture, especially if they are managers, is the other people you will lose. In the three months Tommy spent with us, we lost the whole staff he inherited.

D. Your worst hires will not be smart.

How I missed Tommy's lack of sales ability during the interview process embarrasses me. Then again, the rest of the executive team and the board missed it too.

Tommy had a great background. He came highly recommended, and his reference checks were all good. However, he was a complete disaster.

There was no missing Tommy's lack of skill, once he started working with us. It's still painful for me to think about how unprepared he was.

We all whiffed in hiring Tommy. Scratch that. I whiffed in hiring Tommy.

Tommy was, of all the people I've ever hired, by far my worst hire. He is the only person I've ever hired to be lacking in all four key traits. That's right. Tommy had the really rare Grand Slam of bad traits.

ROUND 6: RAISING YOUR FUNDING IS NOT FOR THE FAINT OF HEART

The Nine Facts of Fundraising
You Need To Know

"Hey Brett, I'm going to be on vacation for the next couple of weeks. I'll pick up the diligence when I get back," Tucker said to me.

Tucker was a potential new investor in our company. I could tell he was serious about investing in our company, based on the work he was doing.

However, it was July. Tucker and his family were going on vacation for a couple of weeks. Therefore, the investment would have to wait.

I replied, "No problem. I look forward to talking to you, when you return."

We had started raising this round in January. We'd already had enough twists and turns for a good Hollywood movie.

I was bummed, but there was nothing I could do to move Tucker along faster. It was summer after all.

Fundraising fact of life number 1: Things do slow down, sometimes, during the summer.

So, what did I do?

I kept working on the other prospective investors we had in the queue.

We had just presented to Jim's partnership a week ago. Jim's firm was proceeding with the final pieces of diligence they needed from us.

Jim wasn't going on vacation. So, I kept working with him.

I wanted a term sheet from Jim. I also wanted a term sheet from Tucker. (We ended up getting term sheets from both Jim and Tucker.)

There were also other potential investors who we could meet with. Therefore, we kept moving as fast as possible, despite it being summer.

Fundraising fact of life number 2: It's likely to take you at least six months or more to raise your funding.

Fund raising takes time, unless you get really, really lucky. You need to plan for at least six months to raise your money.

In our case, we started raising this particular round in January. We received our first term sheet in early May, but we needed more money to close the round.

Therefore, we were still looking for money in July.

Fundraising fact of life number 3: In fact, you

should plan on it taking one year to raise your money.

Then, you'll have a buffer.

I'm glad that we started in January, because all sorts of unforeseen things can happen when you're raising money:

- The economy could go into recession and the funding environment changes for the worse.

- Your company's growth can unexpectedly slow.

- One of your investors changes their mind about accepting an outside investor's term sheet.

- You could lose your 30% customer.

- Your VP of Sales quits.

You get the idea. All sorts of bad, unexpected things can happen, when you run a startup and you are in fundraising mode.

Fundraising fact of life number 4: You are the only one who will have a sense of urgency about closing your funding.

Therefore, you have to push everyone else to the finish line.

It's kind of crazy, because there are millions of dollars at stake. However, you will see that no one but you has any sense of urgency about closing your funding. You would think your investors do, but they don't.

You're just another deal and just a set of numbers to your investors. I know it sounds cold, but it's true.

Your life will change dramatically, if your company ends. Your investors will simply write off your deal and move on.

Fundraising fact of life number 5: It ain't over till it's over.

Baseball hall of famer Yogi Berra said this about the team he was managing (the New York Mets) chances of winning the pennant in 1973, when they were way behind. The Mets eventually won the pennant.

Fundraising is a grind like a baseball season. You are going to lose a lot, but you have to keep getting up and fighting every day, until you win your pennant (funding).

Fundraising fact of life number 6: It ain't over till it's over. Reprise.

You kept grinding and you got a term sheet. You think your work is done, because you've gotten your term sheet.

It ain't over till it's over. In other words, you can still have defeat snatched from victory at the last moment.

Term sheets are non-binding documents. As a result, your new investors can walk away at any time without any recourse.

Remember fundraising fact of life number 4. You are the only one who will have a sense of urgency about closing your funding.

You have to push everyone to the finish line: Your lawyers, the investor(s) lawyers, your investor(s), the new investor(s) and your team.

Have an action plan of everything that needs to get done. Put together as short a closing schedule as possible.

You must then micromanage the process every single day, until the money is wired, safe and sound, into your bank account.

Fundraising fact of life number 7: There's always another round.

It's like the line from Godfather III, when Michael says, "Just when I thought I was out, they pull me back in."

Sadly, there's always another round of money to raise. You have to raise money, even when you're profitable.

Maybe you want a line of credit from the bank?

Maybe you're not quite profitable, so you need to raise one final round of equity?

Maybe you want to IPO.

Fundraising fact of life number 8: The reality is that you are always pitching your company to someone.

One of the realities of life as a CEO, is that you are always selling something to someone.

That key executive you want to hire? You're going to have to pitch your company to the them.

What about that new large customer who you want to add? You're also going to have to pitch them.

Do your existing investors want an update? You are pitching your company again.

Pitching your company never stops.

Fundraising fact of life number 9: The best time to raise money, is when you don't need it.

Investors can smell desperation a mile away. The closer you are to running out of money, the more desperate you are likely to appear.

Desperation leads to bad deals or, worse yet, no deal at all.

Do yourself a favor. Don't wait to raise your next

round, just because it's summer. Get started now, before it's too late.

How Long Does It REALLY
Take You to Get Funded?

"How long do you think it's going to take to get funding?" My wife asked me.

It was January, and we had just started raising money.

"My guess is that we'll be funded by June."

It turned out I was right. We were funded by June... two years later!

We started off our fundraising with a lot of momentum. We had many warm introductions to VCs through the various contacts I had.

A very rare thing happened after one of our first investor meetings. The VC actually called me to pass on the deal.

Then something even rarer happened. He suggested that I pitch to Opus Capital. He said, "I can make the introduction if you'd like. However, it's probably better if you do it yourself, because they'll ask me why I'm passing."

I knew someone who knew one of the partners at

Opus. I thanked him for the tip, and I reached out to the Opus partner I knew.

Two weeks later, we had our first meeting with Opus. By early April, we had a term sheet for $11 million!

I was pumped!

My co-founders were pumped!

I was very confident that we would be able to quickly find another investor. We did get really close with a few potential investors.

It should have been easy, right? We had a term sheet from a very reputable investor and we had a great team. However, we just couldn't get across the finish line.

A. The Great Recession happened.

At the time, you didn't know exactly how bad things were really going to get. However, it was clear that there was a lot of uncertainty out there.

When you see banks, like Lehman Brothers, start to collapse, you know you are in trouble. We were still able to get meetings as the year progressed, but it just kept getting tougher and tougher.

We had one smaller fund that wanted to invest $3.5 million, so we would have been able to get to a total of $9 million. They gave us their proposal in August.

However, Gill, the partner we were working with, didn't want to work with them. When he called to tell me, I knew it was going to be a long, long winter.

Through the winter and the spring of the next year, things really slowed down. The appetite for investing seemed to be about zero.

We could still get meetings, but it almost felt like investors were meeting with us, because they wanted something to do. It was clear they weren't going to invest.

Maybe their thought process was, "I'm taking these meetings with the hope you'll still be around when I can invest."

We didn't give up.

We kept at it.

I added another co-founder to the mix. We also added our only angel investor, Bob.

Bob was a co-founder of one the most successful companies in our space. He was considered a technical genius. It was coup having him on board.

Bob's presence helped. However, the headwinds we faced were still strong because...

B. Investor appetite for funding our type of company (semiconductor) went way down.

The number of investors willing to invest in a Series

A semiconductor company was already low when we started. It dwindled to less than 10 VCs in the Silicon Valley, by the time we closed our funding.

There were fewer and fewer successful semiconductor startups, so it wasn't surprising that more funds were backing off. The partners who specialized in our space weren't being asked to participate in the next fund the VCs raised.

Simply put, they were being asked to retire.

It's funny because you could feel the momentum slowing in our space. At least it felt like the momentum was slowing.

However, we kept going and, over two years after we started, we actually raised $12 million.

What can you learn from my experience? Fundraising is unpredictable.

There are many things that are out of your control, as you can see. The economy and investor appetite are only two of them.

I have a friend who started his company five years ago. The company has made steady progress. His savings are almost gone, yet he is still hanging on, hoping the company will break through.

You might be lucky, like "Evan." I started working with Evan last year, when he founded his company.

Evan had a great idea. However, he was raising

money in a tough space, just like I was. However, in Evan's case, he had multiple term sheets to choose from and he quickly raised his Series A funding of $6 million in five months.

The point is there are many unforeseen things between you and being able to pay yourself.

I like Randall Reade's suggestion on Quora, so I'll copy it here:

"Develop a plan for how much you'll need to live barebones for the next three years, while you work on your company. Then double it."

If you look at my friend's experience, Randall's suggestion is just about right. He's five years in. Hopefully, he'll be able to breathe a little easier in Year Six.

Starting a company is not for the faint of heart.

Financial stress is the just the start. You're going to have to deal with all the stress that comes with not knowing whether this massive bet you've made is going to pay off.

However, having a plan, even if the plan isn't perfect, gives you an idea of how much money and time it's going to take. As you learn more, you can then revise your plan.

What Shouldn't Be In Your Pitch Deck?

"We need to show them (potential investors) how everything functions at the transistor level," our VP Engineering, "John," said to me.

"I don't know," I said. "From what I've seen as an EIR, that will go over the heads of investors." I continued, "But, if you want to do it that way, then go for it. We'll learn whether you're right or not."

We included the detailed engineering description in our pitch. We were doing a practice pitch to two of the partners, Dave and Alain, at the fund where I was an EIR (Entrepreneur in Residence).

We got to the engineering section of the pitch, and Dave, my mentor at the VC fund said, "That's way too much detail. You're going to lose everybody, if you do that."

Amazingly, John still didn't want to believe Dave (who, btw, was a very good engineer with significant expertise in our domain). It was a warning sign that John wasn't going to be working with me much longer.

Getting too much into the technical details, is just one of the things you should avoid doing in your pitch deck. There are many more things you should avoid including:

A. You shouldn't wait to make your key point, until your fifth or later slide.

Attention spans are short. You don't have the luxury of building up a story, and then getting to the meat of the story ten minutes in. Almost everyone in the audience will have lost interest by then.

You have to get there immediately, like in seven seconds or less. That's how fast you have to act.

B. You shouldn't put a lot of text in your pitch deck.

You really want to minimize the amount of text you have in your deck. Why? It is because most people don't like to read text, when they can get more information with a graphic.

This may drive you a little crazy, but graphics are more visually appealing than text is. You want your deck to be inviting to your audience. Too much text gives the signal that your business is too much trouble to understand.

C. You shouldn't use animation in your pitch deck.

You know the old saying that anything that can go wrong will go wrong. That's why you shouldn't use animation, because it will not work at exactly the wrong time.

You can use poor man's animation instead. What is poor man's animation, you ask? Poor man's animation are consecutive slides that give the appearance of animation, without the risk of something breaking.

D. You shouldn't use a fancy template in your pitch deck.

You want the focus of your deck to be your story, not the template. That's why a fancy template is not needed. You can also avoid the cost of hiring a designer.

A plain white background with your company logo in the footer is all you need.

E. You shouldn't use charts for your financials.

I know it looks great to have that chart of your growth that looks like a hockey stick. Instead, you should have a simple pro-forma income statement that gives all the important financial information in one place.

You can just copy and paste from your financial plan (you do have a plan, don't you?). This makes things really easy for potential investors to see exactly what's going on financially with your company in one slide.

Why You Need To Make Your Pitch Helpful To Investors

Dear fellow entrepreneur,

I know you want to knock it out of the park with your pitch. I also know you want to help investors clearly see your vision.

Here are my seven tips for hitting a home run every time you pitch to investors:

A. Know your audience.

Spend the time before you meet with an investor to learn about them. Read the investor's biography on the fund's webpage.

You should also go to LinkedIn and read the investor's biography there. Look at the investments the investor has previously made.

If the investor has done interviews, look them up and read, watch, and listen to them.

All of this work will help you understand who you are talking to. The better you know someone, the better chance you have of receiving an investment.

B. Get to the meeting 15 minutes early.

Investors are notorious for being late. However, you're going to show up early.

Why? It is because you never want to be late to an investor meeting. Just think of being 15 minutes early as your buffer, in case of unforeseen circumstances.

Sometimes, the investor's admin will let you set up early in the conference room you are going to meet in. Get your computer hooked up to the flat screen and make sure that everything is ready to go.

C. After the investor arrives, get down to business fast.

Time is an investor's most important commodity, so start your pitch quickly to be helpful. Yes, shake hands and exchange pleasantries, but you need to get moving.

You might have thirty minutes up to an hour. If the investor was late to your meeting, assume you only have the remaining time to deliver your pitch.

D. You need to sell your business based on your first slide.

Investors make their decisions quickly. You have a limited amount of time, maybe seven to ten seconds, to get the investor you are meeting with excited about your company.

Help the investor make the right decision about

your company, by explaining in the first slide why the investor should invest in your company. You need to explain in the first slide:

- What your company does

- Why your company is 10X to 100X better than anything else

- How big the opportunity you are pursuing is

E. Simplifying your pitch.

Less text and more graphics are always the way to go, when you're pitching. Always be thinking about how you can make it easier for an investor to see what your company's value is.

The simpler and easier it is for an investor to see what you're doing, the more helpful you are being to the investor. Don't try and prove how technical you are. Keep it simple and easy to understand.

This gives you the best chance for success.

F. Have easy to follow, pro-forma financials in your slide deck.

Maybe it's just the entrepreneurs I've been meeting lately, but I've seen this trend where financials are being shown as graphics. I'm old school, and I find it much easier to follow, if your financials are shown in a spreadsheet format.

You can just cut and paste from your financial plan. You do have a financial plan, right?

G. Have your backup slide deck ready.

There's a common list of questions you are going to be asked that don't fit into your deck. Include these slides in a backup deck, so you can help your potential investors get the information they are asking for on the spot.

In this way, the question is fresh in the investor's mind. You have also immediately answered the question. That helps the investor, and it helps give you the best chance of success.

I hope you found my list of the seven steps you can take to make your pitch deck more helpful useful.

Best regards,

Brett

How to Successfully Pitch Your Business In One Slide

I magine this scenario. You're in a meeting with a major potential customer.

This one customer can make or break your business. You have to win this deal, or your business is going to fail.

You can also imagine this scenario. You're raising money.

The potential investor seems really excited about you and your company. This meeting will likely determine your fate.

You can also imagine this scenario. You're recruiting a very talented potential new employee. The potential new employee has asked you to present your plan.

Are you ready? Because you only have seven quick seconds to win or lose the deal, get the funding, or hire the really talented employee.

That's it, seven quick seconds. You may have even less time, if you're pitching to investors.

People make buying decisions very quickly. They

then spend the rest of their time with you justifying their decisions.

What can you do to grab your audience's attention in less than seven seconds?

I introduced my brother to a friend who could be a potential client last week. My friend called me yesterday and said he was going to work with my brother.

Here's what my friend said about his meeting with my brother, "He explained what was going on so simply. It was like I was in the first grade."

You are more likely to succeed, the simpler you make your product and your business to understand for customers, investors and potential employees.

It seems backwards, doesn't it? Your product needs to be complex for others to truly value it, right?

This is the trap that too many people fall into. You end up losing your audience, when you try to show how smart you are.

Introducing the concept of elegant design.

I've been working with an entrepreneur for the past few months. He's preparing to launch his new technology company this summer.

I asked him to explain to me how his product worked. The idea he has is very simple, yet it is incredibly powerful.

I am not a technical expert in what his business will do. However, the power of his idea was easy to understand.

That's elegant design. Elegant design is simple to understand and powerful.

That is what your goal should be, when you explain your business.

Just like my brother or the entrepreneur I am working with, the goal is keeping it simple.

You can start by following this three-step process:

A. Simplify your presentation.

The less technical, the better. One of the most common mistakes entrepreneurs make is overcomplicating their business.

The goal isn't showing your audience how smart you are. The goal is showing your audience how obvious it is that your product and your business are the right choice.

The way you do this, is by making your product and business easy to understand.

B. Practice your pitch to a close friend or relative.

Make sure they are not in your industry and preferably are not technical. Then go through your pitch, except only show them your first slide.

That's right. Only show them your first slide.

All the important information you need to convince an investor, customer, or potential employee to invest, buy, or work with you should be conveyed in that first slide:

What does your product or business do?

Why are you 10X to 100X better than your competitors?

How big is the market opportunity that you are addressing?

C. See if your audience gets how you are unique and differentiated in seven seconds or less.

Finish going through your first slide. It should take about two minutes.

Ask your audience those three important questions:

1. What does my product or business do?

2. Do you think we are better than the competition? By how much?

3. How big is the market opportunity that we are addressing?

You know you've nailed it, when your audience can answer those questions correctly. You're going to have to keep working on your messaging, until you pass this crucial test.

Why is the first slide so important?

The majority of your audience is going to make up their minds based on their initial impressions. Therefore, the first slide and the first moments, are the difference between success and failure.

In other words, your first slide has to do all the heavy lifting. You're going to win over your audience right there, if you get this right.

The rest of your presentation is also important. However, the rest of your presentation just gives your audience more details to support their decision.

Remember this: Tell them what you're going to say. Say it. Then say it again.

Tell them what you are going to say.

This is your first slide: the slide that does the heavy lifting.

Say it.

This is the body of your presentation. You put the facts and data supporting your first slide in this part of the presentation.

Here you will go into more detail to:

- Justify the market size.

- Explain your go to market strategy.

- Go into more detail about your technology in layman's terms.

- Explain who you are competing with and how you are different in a meaningful way to your customers (there's always competition).

- Show why you're the right team to solve this problem.

- Explain your financials.

You can do this in about seven slides. That's not bad.

Then say it again.

This is your conclusion. You are summing up what you previously said.

Warning: Getting your first slide right, is going to take time and many iterations.

Maybe when you start, your messaging might not be perfect. You may also think your messaging is spot-on only to find out that you still need to work on it.

In my case, I don't think we really nailed this for over a year. In fact, we may not have really nailed our messaging, until we were raising our second round of funding, but...

The difference is night and day, when you get it

right!

You could just see the instantaneous understanding, acceptance, and (most importantly) excitement regarding what we were doing. The typical responses were:

"Oh wow. This is really cool!"

"I get it!"

"You guys are in a great position to win!"

Don't get discouraged. Just keep working to get better.

The reality is that making your business easy to understand usually takes a lot of work. In fact, you may work on it for months, only to realize that you're not there yet.

Again, that's okay. You should be constantly working to improve your messaging, so it keeps getting easier for your audience to understand.

And just like in our case, you'll know you have your messaging right when your audience is responding with "Oh wow!" "I get it!" and "You guys are in a great position to win."

What Do VCs Notice When You Pitch Them?

The CEO, who was wearing a polo shirt, sat down in the middle of our big conference room. There were about 10 of us from the fund in the room with him.

The CEO didn't stand up, like the other CEOs present did. Instead, he stayed rooted like a plant to his chair.

That was the first thing I noticed about the CEO of this long-forgotten company. No, he didn't get funding from us.

There was also the CEO of an infamous solar power company (we had a big bet on solar, so we met with just about everyone in the space that was raising money). He was chewing gum and talking really fast.

I just remember thinking this guy is a real character. He wouldn't be taken seriously, except that solar was a hot space back then.

Then there was Josh James, currently of Domo fame. When we met him, he was CEO of Omniture. He was looking to do a PIPE deal (private investment in public equity) with us.

What I remember most, was Josh's presence. You could smell his success.

In short, you remember the CEO.

I can only speak for myself, but you can see the pattern. It's always about the CEO.

This should make sense, because startups are always defined by you, the CEO. Therefore, what are some practical things you should do, if you're going to meet with VCs?

A. Do your preparation before you meet with VCs.

"Here's a slide I think might be good," the CEO said to us.

The CEO had just blown it. I mean completely blown it. We were sincerely interested in investing in the CEO's company.

We liked the technology. We liked the engineering team. However, the CEO was so unprepared, that we couldn't move forward.

You should come to all your investor meetings rehearsed and prepared. Don't expect a VC to move forward with you, unless you're prepared.

B. Arrive to your meetings at least 15 minutes early.

You never want to be late to an investor meeting. With potential traffic issues, you never know if you'll be delayed.

Plan on getting to your investor meetings 15 minutes early, just in case. If you have to go a longer distance, you may want to increase your buffer.

Set up your slide deck before the investor(s) arrive in the conference room. If you do this, you will be prepped and ready to go.

C. You should always have a hard copy back up, just

in case.

My business partner, Cathal, and I had to fly to New York to meet with some investors, who were planning on investing about $80 million, based on our recommendation. We had prepared a slide deck on our computer, a thumb drive with the deck, and, just in case, we also had hard copies of the presentation.

We got to the investor's office about 15 minutes early. To our horror, we couldn't connect either of our computers to the screens the investor had installed in the conference room.

Thank goodness we had the backup hard copy of the deck. We walked the investors through our pitch, using the hard copies we had printed. The deal was closed a few days later.

D. You make your first impressions within seven seconds.

Stand up and extend your hand when an investor enters the room. Smile and look the investor(s) right in the eye. You should also introduce yourself.

This is simple stuff, but it goes a long way.

E. You should use the rule of four, when you're presenting.

What's the rule of four? Easy. You should stand up, if you are presenting to more than four people.

Do you remember my story of the CEO who was stuck to his seat and didn't get an investment? Exactly.

F. You should assume you have half the time you've been allotted for your pitch.

Let's say you have a one-hour time slot for an investor meeting. You should assume you only have 30 minutes for your pitch.

This gives you buffer for Q&A and if the investor is late. Assume you have about two minutes to present each slide. Thirty divided by two means you should have a maximum of 15 slides in your deck.

G. You also need a backup slide deck.

Nothing is better for your credibility, if you can answer all the questions asked during the meeting. However, you should never make things up, if you don't have the answer. It's always better to say you don't know, if you don't have the answer.

However, wouldn't it be great if you did have the answer ready? That's where your backup slides come in handy.

Why Aren't VCs Interested in Investing in Your Business?

One of the worst pieces of advice I ever got was from an investor who told me, "Visit ten VCs. If none of them are interested in investing, then you should quit."

I am so glad that I ignored his advice, because I would have never gotten funded, if I just gave up after meeting ten investors.

You learn pretty quickly that there are many reasons why an investor may pass on your company. You also learn that many of these reasons have nothing to do with you.

Worse yet, most of the time you rarely get good feedback as to why an investor is passing. You're left to figure it out on your own.

What if you have a great idea and you've got some traction in the marketplace. However, the investors aren't interested. There can many possibilities including:

A. Your company isn't in a segment that the investor is interested in.

Are you wondering why you can't get meetings with investors? This could be the answer. It is because not all investors are interested in the same things.

It is important to do your research before trying to set up meetings. You should only try to meet with investors who are interested in what you are doing.

Oh, and also pay attention to…

B. Your company may not be at the stage that the potential investor is interested in.

Investors specialize. There are angels, early stage VCs and late stage VCs. It is important do your research, because it is very difficult to get a mid or late stage VC to invest in your early stage start up.

C. Your company will not move the needle on the potential investors fund.

Let's say you're building a company that has the potential to be worth $100 million. That sounds pretty good, but you need to look at things from the investor perspective.

The $100 million that your company might be worth, will not impact the return for a $1 billion fund. You're better off trying to find smaller funds, where your success can make a huge dent in the performance of the fund.

D. Your company could also not be in the right

geography for the potential investor.

I think this Marc Andreessen quote says it all about the importance of a startup's location regarding fundraising:

"Location risk -- where is the startup located? Can it hire the right talent in that location? And will I as the VC need to drive more than 20 minutes in my Mercedes SLR McLaren to get there?"

So, yeah, location is really important, especially if you are early stage. Investors want to be close to their investments when a company is just starting out.

E. Your company isn't growing quickly enough.

You've bootstrapped revenue up to the magic number of $1 million/year. That's a tremendous achievement.

However, your plan is to grow revenue to $1.5 million next year, then $2.2 million, and then to $3 million the year after that.

That's just not fast enough to get investors excited about your company.

F. Your company takes too much money to get to cash flow positive.

You could have a company that is growing from $1 million to $10 million to $30 million in revenue, but you might not get to cash flow positive, until you get to $200 million in revenue.

That's going to take a lot of money for investors to carry you. Investors are going to have to have faith that there will be another investor willing to continue investing, because there's no hope your company will be able to stand on its own.

G. Your company has no barriers to entry.

You could have a great, growing business that's on the verge of profitability. You could be in an interesting segment, but you have no way to keep competition out of your segment.

That's going to be a tough sell to potential investors.

H. The investors you approached have already invested in a similar business.

It's very rare that an investor will invest at the same time in two similar companies in the same segment. If you take a meeting with an investor that has invested in your competitor, assume your pitch deck will make its way to your competitor.

You get the idea. I can keep going on and on about the reasons why you're not getting funded.

You can have a great business, but it might just not be suitable for venture funding. There's nothing wrong with that at all.

Most businesses are not going to be interesting to VCs. What do most entrepreneurs do in that case? You'll need to do what they do. Rely on your own financing, friends and family, or the bank.

Why Taking Funding Too Early, Can Kill Your Startup

"Equity is like jet fuel for a startup," Gill, one of our investors, said to me one day.

In our case, not only was early stage funding jet fuel, early stage funding was absolutely necessary.

Why? Well, unless you have $20 million-$30 million lying around, it's pretty difficult to build an analog semiconductor company. The numbers go to over $100 million to build a microprocessor company.

That's part of the reason we got funding at all. Building an analog IC company is cheap compared to building a microprocessor company.

Analog companies use trailing edge technology, because analog doesn't scale like digital does. Therefore, our mask costs (the information that's provided to the fabrication facility to make the chip) are orders of magnitude less than digital ICs.

We've answered how funding makes it easier, in some cases essential, to build your company.

What about not taking funding makes it harder for you to build your company?

The downside of taking funding is pretty obvious. You now are beholden to an outside investor.

It doesn't matter if you own the majority of stock, you have to execute, or you will no longer run your company. Therefore, what are the keys to making this relationship work?

You need to be in alignment with your investor(s):

A. You need to be in financial alignment with your investors:

Let's say you take a $1 million seed stage investment, and you give up 20% of your company in return. Your investors are probably hoping to make 30X on their money or $30 million.

For your investors to make $30 million, your company needs to be worth $30 million/20% = $150 million. Welcome to the big leagues.

Was getting to a valuation of $150 million your goal when you started the company, or would you have been happy selling the company for $40 million a few years down the road?

It's pretty easy to see how you can fall out of financial alignment with your investors, if you don't want the same thing.

B. Your vision for the company needs to be the same as your investor(s)' vision.

You have a vision to develop products for Market A using Technology B. Your investors believe you should develop products for Market B using Technology A.

Your investors will likely support you going after Market A with Technology B. However, they will not like it. You may also lose your investor support quickly, if you are not successful quickly.

Don't just take money from any investor.

Investor relationships are long term, seven to ten-year relationships. You need to be in alignment with your investors to make it work.

ROUND 7: WHY TRYING TO MAINTAIN 50% OWNERSHIP OF YOUR STARTUP IS A WASTE OF TIME...AND OTHER LIES

How To Keep From Hiring Superstars That Kill Your Company

I was just having coffee with a friend of mine. I've known Bill for years and I've never seen him this upset.

"You wouldn't believe what my boss just did!" Bill said to me.

"What did your boss do?" I asked.

"They just promoted someone who has no work experience to my level of Director. I was so pissed, that I went to my boss and threatened to quit."

"What did your boss do?"

"He said he would talk to the CEO about promoting me to a level between VP and Director."

I started laughing.

"Why are you laughing Brett?" Bill asked.

"It's a classic maneuver," I said. "You have a bunch of disgruntled employees and you're worried about losing them.

"What do you do? You promote them, so they'll stay. Sometimes it works and sometimes it doesn't work."

"I'm still pissed," Bill said. "I'll take the promotion if I get it, but I don't trust these people (management) anymore."

You lose the trust of your people, when you overpay someone.

Make no mistake about it. You can also overpay someone by non-monetary means. An inflated title certainly fits.

I used to believe the saying "titles are free."

There's no cost to an inflated title, right? You're also making someone feel good.

I worked at a company years ago, where an employee was promoted. Word got around that the employee had quit, and management promoted the employee to keep him from leaving.

It soon became commonplace. A surefire way to get promoted was to quit.

The problem is, what about the people that play by the rules?

You can't promote a fair work environment, when you're not treating everyone in a similar manner.

I had a young employee at the same company. John

had considerable potential, and he was really good.

John wasn't ready to be promoted yet. However, I intended to promote him in a year. I wanted him to earn the promotion, rather than being given the promotion.

I told John during his review what a great job he was doing. I also told John he was a year away from being promoted.

John was crushed.

John couldn't understand why others (through the "I quit" methodology) were being promoted and he wasn't. In John's eyes, it wasn't fair.

John was right. It wasn't fair that he was playing by the rules and not being rewarded.

Your culture takes a beating, when you are not consistent.

This is true every time. Every single time I have overpaid for someone, I have regretted it. Interestingly enough, the same problem happens every time:

The superstar you just hired is never worth it. Ever.

I was looking for a co-founder/VP Engineering, when I started my company. I talked to many people. There was one person that I really liked.

However, I got the feeling that he wasn't going to be

a good partner. He just seemed in it for himself, so I passed.

You're looking for people that are team oriented.

Yes, the person may have a great resume and it may be very tempting. Don't do it. This person is not a good fit for your startup.

Why? Mercenaries who don't care about your team, rarely work out.

An experienced candidate who is a great fit for your company will adjust their salary requirements to what you can pay.

Let me give you an example.

I had worked with Greg on and off for 20 years. Greg is considered one of the gurus of Analog IC design. He's probably one of the 10 best Analog IC designers in the world.

Greg had been working at another company (part time), when we started our company. The company Greg came from was a large public company in the space (kind of a Google equivalent in the Analog IC world). Greg, for various reasons, was unhappy.

We had an open house and Greg came by. We started talking about how we could work together again.

I asked Greg, "What are you currently being paid?"

"$400,000," was Greg's answer.

"You know we can't pay you that. Here's what we can do," I told Greg.

It was over 50% less than he was currently making, but consistent with the salaries we were paying other senior engineers.

Greg agreed to join us.

Greg was great! Not only did Greg develop unbelievably great products, he helped mentor younger engineers, and he helped everyone raise their game.

However, it never would have worked, if Greg wanted to be paid more than the other senior engineers.

There would have been several problems:

- The other engineers would have resented Greg being paid more, and...

- The engineering team and the rest of the company would feel we were not being fair, and...

- Your team will not be loyal (nor should they be loyal), if you're not being fair, so...

- You need to develop the guts to pass.

Your company culture is the most important part of your startup. Your culture is a living and breathing entity that changes each time someone new is hired.

All it takes when you are small is one bad employee for your culture to be destroyed.

Let's say you have nine people, including yourself, on your team. You now have the chance to hire a true superstar, but they want too much money.

You try negotiating with the superstar, but they will not budge. You can sense already that the superstar will be a challenge. However, you really need him.

Should you take the risk?

I'd vote against taking the risk, because now 10% percent of your workforce is problematic. I know you really need the superstar, but there will be other superstars that believe in your company AND fit the culture.

Just remember that it's much harder rebuilding a culture.

You can fire the superstar, if they don't work out. However, your culture has been changed, because you've redefined what's acceptable. It's not okay to hire someone who doesn't fit the culture that you've struggled to build.

You should instead hire smart, passionate people with integrity that fit the company culture you are building. It is true that finding superstars who want to be part of a great team are tough to find.

You're building a great company, right? It takes the courage to say, "No thanks" to the supremely talented superstar who doesn't fit your vision.

Why Working Long Hours Is Not What You Want Your Team To Do

Years ago, I worked for someone that I nicknamed, "The Michelin Man." He earned his nickname because the Michelin Man had the annoying habit of sitting with his arms folded when you talked to him. That made him look like the Michelin Man.

One of the Michelin Man's other annoying habits was that he liked to walk the hallways late in the day with a little notebook. He was looking to see who was in the office, and who had left the office.

In our Friday staff meetings, the Michelin Man would let us know about certain people in our organization were, in his opinion, "leaving early."

Some of the people that the Michelin Man singled out were the most productive employees I had. It was silly and stupid. However, I had to ask employees that were doing a great job to stick around the office.

The singled-out employees were rightfully upset.

You have a choice as a CEO: Do you want to be a clock watcher or a results watcher?

I was usually the first person in the office, and one of the last people to leave the office. That is how it should be, when you're a startup CEO.

It was the way I worked best. I could get my work done in the early mornings, and maybe late in the day (It also didn't hurt that 880 opened up after 7 PM, so I could get home quickly). The middle of the day was meetings and helping the team.

All you should ask of your team, is that they work hard and work smart.

Having people working late to make you feel good, doesn't help the company.

Let's say that you desire a culture, where the team regularly works late into the night. You can get what you want, and you can even feel really good about things. However, working late doesn't equal extreme productivity.

In fact, you're likely to produce another result: burnout.

Running a company is like driving a car. You need to know when to step on the gas, and when to apply the brakes.

Yeah, I know, you're running a startup, but a hard-working team needs a break every now and then. If you run your team hard all the time, they will resent you. As a result, they will not be there, when you really need them.

Therefore, save the inevitable late night and all-night grinds for when you really need them. Learn to cut your team a little slack every now and then. You might also even consider asking your team to go home early once in a while.

When you really need your team to step up, they will have the mental and physical energy to put forth their maximum effort, when you need it the most.

How Should You Tell Your
Team Really Bad News?

"**W**hat happens if we don't get a term sheet in the next six weeks?" One of my employees asked me this during our company meeting.

I had just let the team know that everyone in the company was going to minimum wage for the next six weeks. During our board meeting the previous day, one of our investors told us he wanted to shut the company down.

The request to shut the company down came out of left field. We were doing well, and our fundraising was also going well too.

We already had one term sheet, and we had several other investors who appeared close to giving us another term sheet. In fact, we had just presented to the full partnership of a fund two days earlier, and we were expecting them to give us a term sheet (they did).

Therefore, I suggested to our investors that we put everyone on minimum wage for the next six weeks, so we could play the hand out. It was a Hail Mary pass that I didn't expect them to agree to, but they did.

The hard part was what should I tell our employees.

You need to be fully transparent, when things aren't going well.

I fully expected that we would get at least one more term sheet. However, that wasn't the point.

You have an obligation to tell your team exactly where things stand at all times. We had been sharing the good news and the bad news with our team throughout the company's life.

My answer to the employee's question of what would happen if we didn't get a term sheet in the next six weeks was honesty:

"Assume the company will not exist, if we don't get a term sheet in the next six weeks," I said. It was a tough and sober message.

Now you'd think telling your team that you may not exist in six weeks would cause a panic. It didn't. We didn't lose a single employee during the following six weeks.

We also ended up getting three term sheets.

You build loyalty by being transparent throughout the company's life.

One of the big mistakes that you make as a first time

CEO is being afraid to share the bad news with your team and your investors. Your investors are expecting bad news to happen, so, in some ways, it's safer and easier to share bad news with your investors.

What about your team? Aren't they just expecting the company to succeed?

The key is just be transparent from Day One. Share both the good news and the bad news. Answer your team's questions, so they are educated on what's going on with the company.

If you do this well, you'll end up with a loyal team that will support you during the tough times. I guarantee you that there will be tough times.

That is the payoff. It is the reason why we didn't lose a single employee during our six-week crisis. You will also get the same loyalty from your team, if you're honest throughout your journey.

Can You and Your Team Achieve Work-Life Balance in A Startup?

Years ago, I was invited by a VC firm to a presentation for aspiring startups in the Silicon Valley. We had just been funded, but I wanted to go to listen to some of the featured speakers.

During the Q & A, someone asked the CEO of a company that just went public about how he maintained work life balance. His answer was a classic:

"Work life balance? You can't have work life balance in a startup!"

You could hear by the CEO's tone, that he was really serious about it.

All I could think was, I am glad I don't work with him.

Can you imagine how depressing it would be, if there was only work in your life?

Picture life working with this CEO. Every day, including Sunday, you're working 12 to 16 hours pushing for deadline after deadline.

After each deadline, you're told there's another equally challenging deadline to meet. However, the CEO keeps pushing, and you have no choice but to keep grinding away.

Since it usually takes seven to ten years to get to a liquidity event, you've got a long way to go.

Burnout? Oh yeah, you'll be burned out alright. And it's not just you that's burned out, just about everyone in the company is burned out in this sweatshop.

You can have work life balance, work hard and succeed in a startup.

I've seen it, and I'm sure others have too.

I saw it first during my time at Maxim Integrated Products. The CEO, the late Jack Gifford, was extremely demanding and the pressure was intense. You were expected to work hard, and the standards were extremely high.

You need a release valve for your team.

At the same time, we had fun, laughed a lot and we were all encouraged to take vacations. The accelerator also wasn't always pushed to the floor.

That was one of the greatest lessons Gifford taught me. He told me:

"Think of running a company, like driving a car. You need to understand when to put on the gas, and when to use the brakes."

That release valve was a key to the company's success.

You would go through periods where you were working normal hours, and then there were times when you have to push. However, you knew that there would be downtime coming.

I remembered Gifford's analogy, when I started my own company. Yes, we ran the car hard and floored it when we had to, but we also knew when we needed to apply the brakes.

The Real Truth About
Managing Remote Teams

My daughter, Avery, had an assignment in her first-grade class. She was supposed to see if she could send a paper turtle to every continent in the world.

The first challenge was what Avery would name her nomadic turtle? Avery was into eating goldfish at the time, so the turtle became known as Goldie.

Blossom and I started thinking about who we knew that could help Avery send Goldie around the world. Blossom's godmother lived in Sweden, so Europe was easy.

We knew someone in Peru, so check off South America. Asia? That was easy too. We also had friends in Africa. Australia? We also had that covered.

We thought getting six of seven continents was pretty good for Goldie. "Daddy, I need to find a way to get Goldie to Antarctica," Avery said to me.

Avery started giving me the look with her big brown eyes.

That's when I remembered that Martin, a brilliant

engineer I had worked with years ago, had worked in Antarctica. Perhaps he knew someone?

I contacted Martin. Sure enough, Martin knew that Jen, a "winter-over" (that means you are spending the winter in Antarctica), was stationed in Antarctica right now!

Martin introduced us to Jen, who was happy to help Avery. Goldie could now visit all seven continents!

Goldie opened the door for Martin and I to discuss working together.

Martin asked me what I was up to, so I told him that my company had just received funding about a year ago. Well, one thing led to another, and Martin asked if he could help us.

I was thrilled because Martin is one of the most talented engineers I know.

However, there were two problems:

1. Martin only wanted to consult for us. I don't like hiring consultants to develop your IP. Why? It is because you're likely to lose the IP, when the consultant leaves.

2. Martin wanted to work from home. He lived in Berkeley, and it was, at best, an hour drive to our Milpitas office. Martin would burn out, if he had to come into the office every day.

The good news was Martin had a fully functioning

lab at home, so he could work remotely.

I decided to take the risk with Martin.

I decided to take the risk with Martin, because we had a long relationship. I felt that any time we get from Martin would be good. I also secretly hoped that Martin would become so excited about what we were doing, that he would eventually join us full-time.

Martin began working with us two days per week. Once he started, Martin was working his ass off. He was charging us for two days work, but I knew that it was a long two days.

The two days per week quickly became three days per week.

I had an advantage going in with Martin, because we had known each other for a long time. I knew Martin was likely going to work hard. However, it brought me great comfort, when I saw how hard Martin was working.

I knew we were getting his best.

Martin became a full-time employee within one year.

I never pressured Martin to join us full time. It just naturally progressed.

Martin continued doing great work for us as a full-time employee. About one year after becoming a full-time employee, Martin told me his wife received a Fulbright Scholarship in Uruguay. He was going to move to Uruguay for six months.

Martin asked, "Is there any way I can keep working with you?"

"We'll make it work," I said. I didn't say it, but I wondered, "How?"

The timing couldn't have been worse for us. Martin was defining the most important product in our new product pipeline.

We all believed the product was a home run. However, effective product definition involves close collaboration between the product definer (Martin) and the design engineer.

Could Martin and the design engineer stay joined at the hip, even though they were going to be separated by two continents?

Martin also had other responsibilities beyond the product definition. Martin had to communicate with the other design engineers, the marketing group, customers and sales.

He was now going to have to do all these things effectively from four time zones and a continent away.

A few months later Martin, his wife and their young son went to Uruguay.

The key to successful remote working relationships: Over-communication.

You know the old saying about, "Absence makes the heart grow fonder." One of our investors had another saying, "Keep your supply lines short."

What did he mean by keeping your supply lines short?

The investor meant you take on more risk, when you have a remote team. You are also going to have to compensate for the risk of having a remote team.

You compensate for the risk by over-communicating.

You and your team at headquarters are going to have to:

- Make sure to communicate more with your remote employees.

- Be available at hours that you normally would not be.

Managers are going to have to spend more of their time then they usually would, managing a local team. That's the hidden cost with remote teams.

However, the real burden falls on your remote employees.

Martin, to his credit, understood that he was going to have to take on the extra burden. He bent over backwards over-communicating with everyone. He made himself available whenever and wherever he needed.

The product that Martin defined became the best-selling product in the company's history. Our revenue was over $5 million/year.

Lessons Learned Managing Remote Teams.

We got lucky with Martin. There is no question about it. Martin and I had a history, so this really helped. However, there are takeaways for all of us:

A. Remote employees need to be self-starters.

The self-starting trait is important for any employee. However, it is critical for remote employees.

You will go insane as a manager, if your remote teams are not self-starters. You will spend way too much time managing and cajoling your remote team. Your efficiency will deteriorate, and your remote team will fail. As a result.

B. You will need to over-communicate with your remote team.

You will need to make yourself available at times outside of normal work hours.

You will also need to spend more time communicating with your remote team than your local team. Your extra effort is a prerequisite for having a successful local team.

C. The ultimate success of your remote team will fall on the remote team itself.

Therefore, it is important to choose wisely. Look for the traits of someone who is a self-starter, who over-communicates, who can work independently and is detail oriented.

Your supply lines will be longer with a remote team, but you can still successfully manage them.

What One Critical Thing Do You Not Realize As A Startup CEO?

I was at a lunch meeting with the head of the venture capital fund that was sponsoring me as Entrepreneur in Residence (EIR). I said to Mike, "I know if we get funded, we will succeed."

Mike looked at me and said, "I can think of 100 things that will kill your company." Mike's tone indicated he didn't want to be challenged.

I thought to myself, "What a jerk. Sure, there's the possibility of something going wrong. However, none of that's going to happen to us."

You don't realize how fragile your startup truly is.

Mike was right. I don't know if there are actually 100 things that can kill your company. I certainly don't want to count all the possibilities. That would be too depressing.

However, Mike's sentiment was right. You just don't realize how fragile your company is, when you're just starting out.

Many different things can kill even the best run, best

financed startup, that's staffed with the best people. Don't think for a second that you are immune from these things happening to you.

Here's the one absolutely worst, nightmare inducing scenario for any startup CEO:

You lose your investors support.

There are many ways that this can happen to you. The following is an example.

Shortly after that lunch meeting with Mike, I started raising money. Dave, the partner who was sponsoring us at the firm, then asked me to stop contacting potential investors.

Dave said the partners at the fund had concerns about the investment. He asked me to complete, what he called, some, "Fetch a rock," requests from the partners.

I asked Dave what that meant. He said,

"I throw you a rock, then you bring it back. You think you're done, then I say, 'fetch another rock.' You fetch the rock again. You're asked to keep fetching rocks, until you get tired and give up."

Dave suggested that I might want to look at the possibility of the fund not supporting the investment. He wouldn't give me a reason for the change of heart.

I continued to hope that maybe we could fetch the

rocks and change the partners' minds. Finally, about one month later, Dave explained to me that he was being asked to leave the fund, so he would no longer be able to sponsor the deal at the fund.

Who would have guessed that the partner sponsoring you as an EIR would be forced out? I would have never believed in a million years that would happen. However, it did happen.

Although I was now on my own, I was still very confident that we would be able to get funded. We had a great team and a great plan. What could go wrong?

The loss of support from the VC fund, led to a cascading set of events.

Now that I was free from the VC fund's grip, I started raising money again. Within one month, we landed what would be our first investor.

It was a well-respected fund on Sand Hill Road. We were raising $11 million, and they committed to giving us $5.5 million.

We signed a term sheet with the fund in April. Everyone I knew told me that finding a second investor would be easy, now that we had a first investor.

However, that didn't happen for us because, yet again, external events came into play. This time, the economy took a turn for the worst.

What we didn't know at the time, was that the U.S. was entering its worst financial crisis, since The Great Depression. For about one year, the climate for investing in early-stage companies became toxic.

Everyone turned us down. By everyone, I mean everyone. A total of 63 Investors said no thanks.

We had only two investors left on our list to contact. We had been avoiding both firms, because we had heard negative things about working with them.

When you're down to nothing, you have no choice but to take a chance. We reached out to the partner at the fund (we will call this fund "Donald Ventures"), who was an expert in our space.

Three meetings later, we found our second investor. End of the story, right?

Not so fast.

At first, everything went well between us and our investors. They were happy with our progress, and we continued executing to plan, adding customers and revenue at a good clip.

It became time to raise our next round of funding. Both our investors, Gill and "Raul," agreed to do their pro-rata.

The climate had gotten tougher for semiconductor

companies to find funding, than when we raised our original funding. It took us about three months, and then we received a term sheet.

The next day, I had a call with Gill and Raul.

"I agree to the term sheet," Gill said.

"I agree to the term sheet," Raul said.

All we needed to do was close our funding. If you haven't realized this already, nothing is done until the money is in the bank. We, therefore, started moving as fast as possible to get through the final diligence and get the money in the bank.

About two weeks later, I was meeting with Raul in his office on Sand Hill Road. It was our normally scheduled meeting, before the following week's board meeting.

Seemingly out of nowhere, Raul said to me, "I think we should sell the company."

Raul's tone indicated he was deadly serious. However, I was having trouble processing the words.

My heart rate spiked. I could literally feel my heart beating. In fact, it felt like my heart might explode out of my chest.

"What?" I said.

Raul repeated his demand. "I think we should sell the company. We might raise the flag and put $1 million into the next round, although even that isn't a given.

"I think we should sell the company."

My heart started beating even harder, if that was possible. Raul and I started arguing with each other.

Raul actually seemed to be enjoying my predicament. He was calm, and I just lost it.

Eventually, after about 45 minutes, I left Raul's office. A sense of dread swept over my body.

That sense of dread would stay with me for the next year.

We would have to find another investor to replace Raul, keep the new investor in the deal and keep Gill and his fund happy.

Two months later, we received a second term sheet from a fund based in Boston (Silicon Valley was out as a possible source). Again, I was thrilled.

The sense of dread left my body.

The Boston investor knew about Donald Ventures not supporting their portfolio companies. Therefore, they added a clause demanding that each existing investor put in a minimum of $1.5 million. Raul blocked the deal, saying his fund would only put in $1 million.

Raul again renewed his demand that we sell the

company. My sense of dread came back again.

However, we had three other investors who were pretty close to giving us term sheets. I felt confident that we would be able to close another investor.

The challenge now became finding a third new investor, while keeping the new syndicate intact. We weren't so fortunate. The Boston-based investor smelled something was wrong, and they withdrew their term sheet.

I still felt confident we could thread the needle and get the two other potential investors to invest. One was a fund based in Pennsylvania, and the other was a strategic (a public company in our space) based in Texas.

About two months later, we were able to get both new investors to commit. We had a term sheet that required none of Donald Ventures' money.

We were home free, or so I thought. Raul blocked this term sheet too, again demanding that we sell the company.

There was one trick I had left up my sleeve. It was a hail Mary pass, but, maybe just maybe, it would be caught.

We had a loan with Silicon Valley Bank. Maybe SVB would step in and help us, because they were going to lose a sizable amount of money.

We had an emergency board meeting scheduled for

the next day. During the board meeting, Raul called Gill to let him know that Donald Ventures would allow the deal to go through.

We had been saved. The sense of dread I had been living with for the past year, left me.

For the next few days, I was euphoric. I was busy doing everything I could to close the money as fast as possible.

Unfortunately, it wasn't fast enough. The first new investor, who had stayed in the deal for eight months, decided to pull out of the deal.

Who could blame them? Raul had created so much uncertainty, that the new investor was worried about Donald Ventures being on the cap table in any capacity.

We tried to save the deal, but we couldn't. Raul had won. We would have to sell the company.

The moral of the story is that there are many unforeseen things that can kill your company.

Little did we know at the time that Raul and Donald (the head of Donald Ventures) were fighting. Raul, not surprisingly, lost the fight. He was told by Donald to liquidate his investments. We were just collateral damage.

I would have never thought we would get tripped up by the problems the partner leading the deal had inside his fund. We did not once, but twice!

The point is that startups are fragile. You hopefully will not go through the ordeal we went through, but you will have challenges that could go either way.

The only thing you will have that will get you through, is your grit.

ROUND 8: EXECUTING YOUR PLAN WOULD BE EASY IF ONLY EVERYONE DID WHAT THEY SAID THEY WOULD DO

What Is the Most Difficult Part About Building Your Startup?

"The hardest part of building our company will be raising the initial funding," I naively said to my fellow co-founders. Every one of them nodded their heads in agreement.

I continued with my pep talk. "We'll be home free, once the funding closes. We've built businesses like this before. We know what we're doing, right?"

I said those remarkable words to the team in January. It would take two more Januarys before we closed our funding. That's two years, if you're counting.

What could be more difficult than your fundraising taking two years?

I was brimming with confidence after we got through our fundraising ordeal. It was 2010. The Great Recession was ending, and I felt like we had the wind at our backs.

The first few months after our funding closed, things seemed to be going to plan. Our recruiting and product development efforts were on schedule.

Our board meetings were a breeze. The investors were happy with our progress. The bumps in the road were just that, bumps.

Six months into our journey as an operational company, I had to fire one of my co-founders. "Randy's" problems working with the rest of the team had become unbearable.

I let the board know I was going to terminate Randy. They were all very supportive. When Randy left the company, it felt like a black cloud had been lifted.

Randy's termination was as rough as things got in those early days. I was disappointed that things didn't work out, but letting him go was the right thing to do.

Achieving traction might prove more difficult than your initial fundraising.

I was meeting with one of our investors, "Raul," in his Sand Hill Road office, right before we released our first product. Raul said to me, "Our conversations will grow more interesting after you introduce your products."

I smiled and nodded. Raul had a reputation for being really difficult to deal with. He'd been fine to deal with since we closed our funding, but I knew he was right.

What would happen if our products didn't gain traction as quickly as we planned?

That's exactly what happened. Our first product was a soft launch, meaning we didn't do any marketing at all. That would come with our second set of 15 products we announced three months later.

The products sold, but not nearly at the pace we had planned on. Sure enough, my conversations with Raul did get more interesting.

Raul: "Why aren't the products ramping?"

Me: "They are, just not at the pace we expected."

Raul: "I'm 79 years old. At this pace, I'll be dead before they ramp. You've got to try something different. Maybe we should come out with lower priced products."

It felt like a panic move to me.

Me: "That's an interesting idea. I'll look into how we can do that."

It would take us over 12 months longer to get to where I expected us to be after six months in the market. Raul kept on me, until revenue finally turned the corner.

Raising your next round of funding and fighting with your investors might prove more difficult than your initial fundraising.

We started raising our next round of funding about two years after we closed our first round. As part of the process, Raul asked me to present an update to his partners.

However, I sensed there might be trouble, because Raul had previously told me the funding was approved and I didn't need to present to the partnership.

I wondered what had changed, so I asked Raul.

"Brett, this should be fine. Make sure to emphasize the low pricing aspect of the business, and don't spend much time on the proprietary business." Raul commanded.

We did implement the family of low-priced products that Raul suggested. It's essentially identical to another family of products we have, but with reduced specifications and prices.

It was an idea worth trying, but we had just put the products in the market, so we didn't have any evidence it would work.

"OK, I understand. I'll review the presentation with you later in the week." I didn't feel comfortable with what Raul was asking, but he knew his partners better than I did.

I still didn't feel comfortable with the direction, but I rehearsed, rehearsed and rehearsed some more, until I felt okay about it. I still had this lingering feeling that something was wrong, but I kept plowing ahead.

I talked to Dave (my advisor) about it. Dave's advice was to follow Raul's instincts, because he knew his partners. Dave had been a VC, so I thought this was good advice.

When I got to the office of the venture fund that Raul worked at, "Donald Ventures," the morning of the presentation, I was escorted into the main conference room. Raul joined me a couple minutes later. We started talking.

"Brett, remember that Donald doesn't care about gross margin. Donald only cares about the top line, so emphasize our new low-price strategy."

My doubts about emphasizing price again popped into my mind, but I pushed them back. It was too late to change our focus.

Raul and I continued chatting. Slowly, but surely, the partners started filing into the conference room.

"Jim," one of the only partners I recognized, had his assistant bring him his tea in a grand show of power. We were still waiting on Donald to enter the scene.

Finally, at 9:15 AM, Donald arrived. His eyes were darker than usual, and his face was bruised (Donald had fallen after waking up over the previous weekend). As usual, Donald sat, slouched as always, directly across from me.

I began my presentation. "Just to update everyone, since I see a lot of new faces here (one of the unique dynamics of Donald Ventures is the revolving door of partners, and that is unusual for a Silicon Valley VC firm), Touchstone is a high-performance analog company. It's a great business model with lots of customers in many different markets...."

Before I could continue, Jim cut me off. "Brett, what is your revenue plan for the year?"

"$1 million."

"What was your original plan?"

"Um, $3 million."

"Wow! One of Raul's companies, not on plan!" You could hear the sarcasm dripping in Jim's voice. In the moment, I thought to myself, "what have I gotten myself into? An internal squabble between Jim and Raul?"

It only got worse from there. It was an ambush. It was, by a wide margin, the worst investor meeting I've ever had.

The funding we had been promised went away in an instant. Instead, Raul and Donald Ventures became obstructionists, trying to force us to sell the company.

The next 12 months proved to be the most difficult of my career. Raul blocked every term sheet we received from closing. It was a nightmare that I would have never expected.

The reality is you just don't know what the most difficult part of building your company will be.

I remember saying to myself, "I just want to breathe." What I meant was that I want to feel like I could relax and exhale, if just for a moment.

The reality is you can, and you should exhale a lot. Meditation helps. Sleep also helps. It also helps to have someone to talk to that you can trust.

The reality is that you are always going to be dealing with something difficult. This is true even when your company is profitable and has made it.

How Can You Prevent Your Team From Misleading You?

"**I** don't want you to attend the weekly sales meeting anymore," our new sales VP, "Tom," said to me. I didn't argue with him, but I was concerned. I'll get back to why I was concerned later.

It seems there is a common belief that the proper way for a CEO to manage, is through a command and control structure. The CEO meets with his or her lieutenants and tells them what to do.

The lieutenants tell their troops what to do and reports the results back to the CEO. There is minimal interaction in this model between the CEO and the troops.

That might work well in the movies. However, command and control doesn't work very well in the startup world.

The best CEOs I've worked with regularly interacted with all levels of the organization. These CEOs would meet with the department heads and staff regularly.

One of the biggest challenges you have as CEO, is the quality of the information you are receiving. As well intentioned as people may be, everyone has biases. A smart way to counteract any biases, is by talking to many different people at various levels of your company.

You can do this through the old Hewlett-Packard management technique called "management by walking around." This simple strategy is just as you'd guess. You just walk around the building and start talking to people.

I found management by walking around a great way to build rapport with your team. It is a great way to have informal conversations on various issues that your company faces.

The second way to improve the quality of information you receive is through meetings. The meetings I liked attending regularly were:

A. The weekly executive staff meeting.

This meeting was just with my direct reports. The goal was to update the team on key issues facing the company, and for the executives to update each other on the progress in their departments.

B. 1:1's with each member of your executive staff.

You want to meet with each direct report individually to provide any necessary coaching or guidance.

Your direct reports can and should also ask for any needed help.

I always thought of these meetings as "mini-reviews" where you are giving the executive instant feedback on what's working. It's a great way to keep the lines of communication open.

It's a red flag, by the way, if your direct reports are not, from time to time, asking for help. It can mean they are trying to hide information from you, or it can mean they are afraid to reveal information to you. Either way, you likely have a problem.

C. All hands meetings with your whole team.

You will learn the hard way, that if you don't give your team information, they will make up the information. For example, if you don't tell your team what last month's revenue is, they will guess the number themselves.

Your team's imagination will run wild, when you don't provide information. For example, your team will think layoffs are coming or that revenue is low. Who knows what might be dreamed up?

The way you combat this, is by having regular all hands meetings with the team. I liked having this meeting the day after our board meetings.

We would go through the open session part of the board meeting; with each department head presenting the same material that we presented to the board. I would talk about the general health of the company, and we would answer any questions the team had.

The team now feels like they know what's going on. You also get a feel for what concerns your team has. Just like in your 1:1 meetings with your direct reports, it's a red flag if no one is asking you tough questions.

Don't worry about information getting beyond the room (it will), because it's worth the loyalty you are building by being transparent.

D. Departmental meetings (when necessary).

You'll want to attend some departmental meetings on an as-needed basis. The value of attending departmental meetings is three-fold:

a. You are showing how important a given area is to the company.

For example, you just introduced your first product to market. You want to show the sales team how important their function is to the company.

You do this by going to the department meeting. You'll let the department head run the meeting, but you'll participate in the meeting, by asking questions and moving the meeting along as needed.

Your team knows their work, if you handle yourself properly in the meeting, has the support of the CEO.

That's important.

b. You are making sure this key area of the company is working well.

You can't sit idly by waiting for the results to come, because the feedback loop will take too long. You need to be actively involved in key areas of the company to keep them moving in the right direction.

c. You are showing your support for the department head.

If you attend a departmental meeting and you contradict the departmental head, then you are doing the wrong thing. The department head will be upset, and rightfully so.

However, you should be on the same page as the department head. After all, you have regular 1:1's with the department head. Therefore, any differences of opinion should be worked out in your 1:1 meeting.

By going to the meeting and supporting the department head you are demonstrating that you and the department head are working together. The team will likely respond well to this synergy.

That is why I was concerned about Tom. I wasn't going to the meeting to spy on Tom. I was there to help and support Tom.

My concern about Tom was correct. Tom missed every revenue goal he set. He was quickly out of the company.

Think of the various areas of your company like a wheel with spokes.

Each department in the company can be thought of like a spoke on the wheel. Your focus will be on some of these spokes (but not all of them) at a given time.

As time goes on you will then focus on other areas (departments) of the wheel (the company). When you are focusing on these areas, you will likely meet with and attend meetings with all levels of that department.

When the department is in steady state, you will likely not attend these meetings. You will move your focus to another area of the company.

That is what good, hands-on, CEOs do to keep their companies executing at a high level.

What Can You Do to Thank Your Team?

Yes, absolutely say thank you to your team. However, that's just the start. There's plenty you can do to make sure your team knows how much you care about them:

A. How about a Starbucks gift card for everyone when you hit a milestone?

Here's a smart thing you can do, so your team can

see their progress. Show a simple graph of the various milestones (small and large) versus time.

Each time you hit a milestone, give your team a token of your gratitude. For small awards, something like a $10 Starbucks gift card or movie tickets is nice.

For larger milestones, think bigger. It could be a cash bonus for everyone. It could also be a group outing.

Now that we've covered rewards, there are other, super important things you can do to reward your employees, including:

B. You should hire only smart people.

You can pay people well and you can give them a lot of time off, but great people want to work with other great people. You have complete control over this, with your hiring standards.

Hire smart people in their respective disciplines. It a big motivator for your team to come into work and actually want to work with the people on their team.

And to that end…

C. Give your team interesting work to do.

You want to build a commitment work culture, where your team never wants to leave. How do you do that?

There is a piece of the puzzle about paying employees fairly and you also want to hire great people.

Another key piece of the puzzle is the work that your employees are doing. Smart people want to work on meaningful things. Let me give you an example.

I was fortunate to work with some brilliant engineers during my career. One of the best was Dave Bingham. Before I worked with Dave, he was General Electric's Scientist of the Year. He was unbelievably creative.

Dave was also unbelievably pragmatic. Any time we discussed a new product, one of Dave's questions was always, "Will it sell?"

Most of the great engineers I have worked with were similar to Dave. They wanted to make sure they were working on something that would sell.

Then...

D. Delegate, delegate, delegate!

There is the old-school, command and control, method of management that is very demoralizing for smart people.

You should instead delegate down in your organization as much as you can. Delegation gives your team higher-level work to do, which is very motivating for smart people.

Delegation also has the extra benefits of giving you the ability to do more higher-level work. It also allows you to be the teacher to your team.

Delegation also gives you the ability to provide guidance to your team about the decisions they are making. Now things are supercharged...

E. Purge your company of any non-performers.

No matter how much you focus bringing in great people, you are likely to hire people that just don't cut it. You have an obligation to the rest of your team to get these people out of the company.

I know it sounds cold (and it is), but problem employees, especially in a small company, cause oversized problems for the rest of the team. There's no bigger morale destroyer, than when you have to cover for your co-worker on a big project.

Firing people sucks. Make no mistake about it, it's on you when someone doesn't work out. However, you have to do it.

Just remember to carry yourself with class and grace when you have to let someone go.

As you can see, saying thank you is more than just saying thanks. You truly show your employees you appreciate them, by building a great company.

How Much Should You Delegate to Your Team as CEO?

I love the idea of obsoleting myself. In fact, the idea of obsoleting myself has been my goal ever since I started managing people years ago. This is because only when you obsolete yourself, can you effectively delegate.

Huh?

Why would you want to make yourself not needed anymore? What does this have to do with delegating to your team?

The concept of obsoleting yourself is somewhat of a leap of faith. You are betting that there will be higher-level work you can do, by having your team be able to do the work.

Leverage is where it's at as CEO.

As CEO, you have to be thinking about how you get your team to do as much as possible. In fact, your goal should be that your company runs perfectly, if you are not involved.

There are two very practical reasons you want to work hard to delegate to your team:

A. You could leave the company.

Stuff happens. There is the real possibility that you will not be with the company at some point. After all, none of us will live forever.

You should want your company to go on seamlessly without you. The only way that will happen, is effectively delegating to your team.

Having a team capable of carrying the load frees you up to do the work that only you can do. That's your goal.

That leads directly to the second practical reason you want to delegate to your team:

B. Delegation allows you to do things only you, the CEO, can do.

You can stay very busy as CEO and accomplish very little, if you're not careful. It is really easy to get comfortable doing tactical work that your team can do.

That's why you need to aggressively delegate to your team:

- Delegating frees you up to do things only you the CEO can do., and...

- Delegating gives you the time to do those things only you can do, and...

- Delegating motivates your team, because

your team will work on higher level stuff.

The problem is you don't have leverage, when you're just starting.

When you're starting out, it's just you and a few others. There is no one to delegate to, so what do you do?

You and your teammates essentially divide up the work.

Your role, as the CEO, is to focus on what your expertise is. You focus on engineering, if you're an engineer. You focus on marketing, if you're a marketing expert.

At the start you are an individual contributor AND the CEO. Over time, you will become just the CEO.

When do you make the transition to just being CEO? A word of warning:

You are on the wrong path, if you think that being the CEO is all about your team doing everything, while you sit back and pass judgment on the work your minions are doing.

That's not what being a great CEO is about.

You do want to leverage your team as much as possible. However, your goal is freeing yourself up to do the work that only you, the CEO, can accomplish. Then you can focus on the big picture issues.

The reality is you'll be transitioning, or should have a mindset of transitioning, from the day you start.

There is no one to delegate to when you're just starting out, so you do the work.

You do what's needed. You'll do everything from working on your core expertise to taking out the trash. It's all hands on deck at the start.

Then you start adding people:

- Engineers typically come first., then....

- You'll probably add a controller/finance person pretty fast, then...

- You'll add manufacturing, if you're making a physical product, then...

- You'll add marketing, as you get ready to sell your product, then...

- There will probably be some inside sales-people, and finally...

- You'll add salespeople last.

Why do you add salespeople last?

Let me clarify this a bit. You might add a pure sales-person or two, but you'll want to wait on adding a VP of Sales because:

It's tough at first to find a really good sales VP.

The reality is that a great VP of Sales is just not going to be interested in joining your company when revenue is low. You're going to be the best salesperson your company has.

You are the one with the most passion about your business. You know the ins and outs better than anyone else.

Therefore, it only makes sense that you are the one selling. There is another huge benefit you get, by being the company's first salesperson.

You know how the sales process in your company works.

You know what the selling process looks like. This is important since you will do a much better job hiring a VP Sales that fits what you truly need.

Don't make the rookie mistake of not staying involved, once you have no more line responsibilities.

Just because all the line functions in the company are filled, doesn't mean you aren't involved in the day-to-day company responsibilities. You don't get to sit back and watch your team work.

It is true that your team will be doing more of the work (freeing you up to do other work only you can do). However, they will be working based on the goals that you and the team set.

You'll be constantly monitoring the various parts of the organization through review meetings. You're also going to be having regular 1:1's (I used to like to do this weekly) with your direct reports.

Oh. One other bit of advice is giving your team the room to make mistakes. Making mistakes and then learning from the mistakes is a key part of how people learn and grow.

The trick as a manager is letting your team make small mistakes. However, at the same time, don't let your team make any company killing or career mistakes. You need to step in, before anything drastic happens.

You are often happily surprised to find that your team not only executes well, but actually comes up with a better way of doing things. That's why you hire really smart people and let them run.

You now know the tricks of effective delegation. Remember to keep the long-term goal of obsoleting yourself in mind, as your company grows. You'll then have the leverage you need to work on the things only you as the CEO can do.

Learn How Using Empathy
Gets the Ultimate
From Your Team

"There are a lot of negotiators that really will give in on a deal, because being understood is more important than getting what they want." Chris Voss, the FBI's former lead hostage negotiator said.

In fact, the first thing master-negotiator Voss teaches, is you need to empathize with your counterpart on the other side.

Say that again? Voss was negotiating with kidnappers and terrorists, and he said empathy is the most important thing?

How on earth can you empathize with a terrorist or a kidnapper?

My goodness, why would you empathize with killers? There just is no way you can do that. Here's the thing about empathy.

- Empathy doesn't mean you agree with where the other side is coming from.

- Empathy does mean you try and show the other side you understand where they are coming from.

That's a huge difference. The other side will be willing to communicate with you, if they believe you understand them.

And why will a terrorist, kidnapper, or an employee believe you understand them?

Let's say you go the extra mile. You truly make the effort to understand the other side. You will then be able to explain the other side's feelings and position in their words.

Your employees will also feel empowered, when they know they are being heard. I'll get back to this point later.

That is why empathy is a business superpower. This doesn't apply to just salary negotiations or customer contract negotiations.

It turns out that empathetic leaders are the most effective leaders.

I've worked for four CEOs in my career. Only one of the four was an empathetic leader.

He truly cared about the people working for him. He also tried to understand the people working for him.

You could see that the CEO's sincerity was genuine.

The CEO went out of his way to make sure his team was taken care of. He cared about everyone that worked at the company, whether you were the lowest level employee or a senior executive.

You're now probably thinking this empathetic CEO was a wimp.

On the contrary, the empathetic CEO was as tough as nails.

Arguing was encouraged. Sometimes the arguments were really heated.

However, there was safety in the environment, because there was empathy. That is what allowed us to argue so strongly for our positions.

Empathy is about being heard. It's also especially important that your team know they've been heard, when you disagree.

It will give your team the power to come back to you and tell that you're wrong. That's right. You want your team to tell you when you're wrong.

Your superpower empathy gives your team the courage to debate and challenge you. That's exactly what you want.

You want to build the best company possible. The startup culture that gives your company the best chance of success is a commitment culture.

The commitment culture is all about your team enjoying what they are doing so much, that they never want to leave. Your team has a much better chance of staying together, if they feel they are being heard.

In other words, you'd better be empathetic, if you want to build a great team that will stay together through thick and thin.

Empathy is the glue that allows your diverse team to flourish.

Slack's CEO, Stewart Butterfield is a big believer in the power of empathy. "When we talk about the qualities we want in people, empathy is a big one," Butterfield said.

"If you can empathize with people, then you can do a good job. If you have no ability to empathize, then it's difficult to give people feedback and it's difficult to help people improve. Everything becomes harder." Stewart Butterfield, CEO, Slack

You can't fake empathy.

Years ago, I worked for a CEO who was the polar opposite of the tough, yet empathetic, successful CEO I talked about earlier.

You had read in interviews with the CEO about how he considered the employees all part of his family and how much he cared about everyone that worked for him.

This CEO showed, in many ways (down to making salaried employees take time off for doctor's visits), that he was the only person he cared about. The results were predictable:

- Employee morale was low., which led to...

- High employee turnover, which led to...

- A company that underperformed the market, which led to...

- The CEO eventually having to sell his company.

What can you do to improve your empathy skills?

It seems simple. All you have to do is listen.

Being empathetic is a lot more than just listening. Listening is just the start. I'll start with some don'ts:

A. Don't interrupt.

Let the other side talk. Men, in particular, have the really bad habit of interrupting.

I know I am constantly fighting my urge to interrupt someone. You know what works for me? Sitting on my hands! Somehow or other sitting on my hands triggers my brain not to interrupt. Then...

B. Make eye contact.

Look directly at the other person, if you are face to face. Don't let yourself be distracted.

Don't surf the net or let yourself be distracted, if you are having the discussion over the phone. Stay focused on the other side.

C. Listen some more.

You should really make sure the other side has said everything they want to say.

My most important piece of advice is:

D. Don't give any advice.

Men are especially bad at this. I thought I was a really good listener early in my career.

Maybe I was. However, I used to blow it, by giving advice right after someone had poured their heart out to me.

That's not what the other side wants or needs. The other side needs to be heard. No matter how well intentioned your advice might be, it does not signal that you really understand someone.

How does someone know they've truly been heard?

Let's go back to master negotiator Chris Voss. Voss outlines a whole sequence that you should follow in his fantastic book, *Never Split the Difference*.

I highly recommend that you read *Never Split the*

Difference. However, I'll do my best to summarize how you can indicate to the other side that you hear what they are saying:

A. Start by mirroring.

Use the language your employee is using to explain their problem. Mirroring indicates that you are really listening to what they are saying.

B. Add in non-definitive statements.

Use phrases like "It seems like," when you are trying to form tentative conclusions. The most important part is C.

C. You have to really care about your team.

Voss' steps for effective communication are simple. However, you can't just say the words. You have to believe what you are saying.

You can't fake empathy. However, you need to master empathy, if you and your company are going to succeed.

The best CEOs understood that being empathetic doesn't mean you can't be tough and demanding. In fact, being empathetic is the secret sauce that allows you to push you and your team to incredible success.

What The Dead Plant Outside Your Office Is Really Saying About Your Company?

I remember walking into the lobby, like it was yesterday. I was excited because I was wrapping up negotiations to join the company as VP Marketing.

I remembered seeing a planter with a dead plant outside. I didn't think much of it at the time. Maybe I should have.

I went into the lobby, and there was the receptionist. I told her I was there to meet the CEO.

She escorted me to the CEO's office, and the CEO greeted me warmly. We had been negotiating for weeks over equity.

The CEO and I came to an agreement on the equity.

I agreed to join the company as Vice President, Marketing.

I joined the company and started evaluating the company's business. One of things that attracted me to the company was the customer base.

Cisco, Lucent and Nortel were customers. The company was doing business with all the big telecom companies of the day.

I was excited, until I started digging into the quality of the business we were getting. All of the customers were using us for prototypes, not production.

There was no way the company could grow, and I knew it. It was startup failure.

Every Friday I had lunch with the CEO. I told the CEO we were going to have to make significant changes, if we were going to grow.

The CEO listened intently each week. Each week he committed to making changes.

Each week nothing changed.

The decision to join this company turned out to be one of the worst decisions I made in my career.

Within three months of joining the company, the CEO was fired. I told the board of directors I wanted to be CEO. I presented my vision for the company to the board, but the board went with an outside candidate as CEO.

I was fired three months later.

I could have seen the company was not well run. After all...

How can you run a company well, if you can't even

water a plant?

Years later, we were raising money, and we were getting close to closing one of the potential investors. They wanted to meet with us at our office.

We had several plants scattered around the office, including one in the lobby. Our VP Engineering and co-founder, Jeroen, had brought the plants in when we moved into the facility. He had done a great job of keeping the plants looking nice.

However, there were some leaves that looked like they were dying, so I went with a scissors and cut all the dead leaves. We weren't going to lose a potential investor over a plant.

One of the engineers, Maurice, had removed the florescent light over his workstation because he didn't like it. I explained to Maurice that we needed the light back in, because we had investors coming to visit.

I assured Maurice that he could take the light out, once the investors left.

Were we putting on a show? Your goddamn right we were!

First impressions matter!

Is your facility clean?

Plants?

Light fixtures?

Bathrooms?

Your lobby?

The chairs?

Your kitchen?

They all matter.

How do you answer the phone?

I remember years ago, when I was working at Maxim Integrated Products. This was in the ancient times when voicemail was just coming into existence.

We were starting to get complaints from our field salespeople and customers regarding leaving messages for people. There was a clamor that the company needed a voicemail system.

Jack Gifford, Maxim's very frugal (I mean this in a very complimentary way) CEO, had another idea. Gifford didn't want to spend on voicemail.

Instead every employee received an answering machine on his or her desk. These were very special answering machines, because they had one, instead of two, cassette tape.

You're asking, why is that important? Well, if you only have one cassette that means your message of, "Hi, I'm away from my office" is on the same cassette as your messages.

Here's the problem with one-cassette answering machines: The tape has to wind from your message at the beginning of the tape to the last message, before someone could leave a message.

Someone could literally wait several minutes for the tape to wind! There was no on hold music, just those tapes winding.

I can still remember walking through the office hearing the sound of those tapes rewinding. You knew whoever was on the line, waiting for the beep to leave their message, had to be frustrated!

Yes, Gifford was very frugal, but he wasn't stupid. I am pretty sure we got a proper voicemail system pretty quickly after the answering machine debacle.

What about your website?

Think of your homepage, like the lobby to your office.

Is your homepage inviting, clean and easy for someone to understand what your company does? Or is your homepage a cluttered mess?

A cluttered homepage is like having dead plants outside your office. And we already know where that leads.

What the most important area that determines the

success of a McDonalds franchise?

Clean bathrooms.

You may not be operating a McDonalds, but your team, potential new employees and customers all are using your bathrooms.

So, maybe your bathrooms really are important? Hmmm.

The list goes on and on.

Business on many levels is not rocket science.

It's the attention to these small details that can make or break your company. Attention to detail doesn't take intellect. Attention to detail is all about caring about the little things.

The funny thing is attention to detail doesn't cost you much money. Most of the time attention to detail actually saves you money.

Who wants to work where there are dead plants in the lobby, or where there are dirty bathrooms?

What are the little details you're overlooking?

ROUND 9: MARKETING AND SELLING YOUR PRODUCT IS NEVER EASY, SO GET READY TO PIVOT

How Do You Define Product Market Fit?

There's a great quote that U.S. Supreme Court Justice Potter Stewart said about obscenity. He said, "I know it, when I see it."

The same can said about Product Market Fit from my experience. You know it when you see it.

When we started selling our products, I had visions of our products instantly flying off the shelf. Things didn't exactly work out that way. Our revenue ramp was much slower than I expected it to be.

However, I knew that we had achieved some sort of product market fit, when we had ten customers buying our first product.

The revenue from those ten customers was only $130. We weren't going to get rich if we kept this pace up, because our goal was getting to $10,000 per customer per year. However, I knew from experience that we were on our way.

How could I be so sure?

The reality is that I was still full of concern and fear. I was constantly asking myself:

"Would the ten customers turn into 100 customers?"

"Would the 100 customers turn into 1,000 customers?"

I knew we were on our way with those first ten customers. All the leading indicators were pointing towards success:

The first leading indicator of product market fit is:

Our model was a broad-based distribution fulfillment model. We needed to get the word out to many potential customers.

Getting the word out, meant primarily spending money on Google AdWords. We added in some focused PR, and it worked.

Our web traffic started growing at a sizable clip. Check.

The second leading indicator of product market fit:

Getting traffic to our website was step one for us. We then needed to get customers to order free samples of our products.

We, therefore, put simple links to our sample page where, in exchange for giving us information about what they were building, their company and their email address, we gave customers free samples of products.

More good news!

Customers were using free samples of our product, in direct proportion to the growth in website traffic. We were selling hardware (analog ICs), but it could be thought of as a freemium model for software.

Once we had customers using the product, we started talking with our potential customers. This led to:

The third leading indicator of product market fit:

The big fear that you have in the world of Analog ICs, is that customers will order samples of your product, put them in a desk drawer and never use the samples.

We needed orders and positive customer feedback to confirm that we were on the right track.

The feedback from our customers was positive. Many customers identified flaws in the product but said they would use the product despite the flaws.

It's a great sign when customers indicate they will use a product despite the problems. That's when you know you are on to something.

Sure enough, ten customers quickly led to 100 customers. 100 customers led to 1,000 customers. The revenue per customer also increased significantly from where we started.

You need to identify your leading indicators of product market fit.

Our business became very predictable as time went on. We knew that X visitors to the website, would lead to Y number of sample requests and that would lead to Z number of customers. You could set your watch to it. That's product market fit in my business.

However, it doesn't mean you don't pivot along the way.

Of course, we pivoted. Every company pivots. They were small pivots and not let's throw out everything we've done and start from scratch type pivots.

The key in the early stages is identifying some key metrics to achieve. As long as you are achieving those key metrics, you are on the right track to achieving product market fit.

How Do You Find Your First Customers?

"How do you intend to market your first product?" one of our board members asked me.

It was March and we were going to launch our first product, the TS1001. We had 20 more products scheduled for launch in June. That was the big event.

"We're going to soft launch," I said. In other words, no marketing, no nothing. We just wanted to make sure that all of our systems were functioning properly before the big June launch.

"Build it and they will come," the board member said in response. Then he added, "I hate build it and they will come."

I replied, "So do I."

I honestly didn't know what to expect. Would anybody even know we existed? We were still in stealth mode, for all practical purposes.

The website was still a crappy GoDaddy edited page. The new website was being readied for the

June launch.

About 24 hours after we soft launched, we received our first order. It was for $13!

You would have thought that we made $1 million from the commotion around the office that day.

Think logarithmically about growing your customer base.

We immediately started advertising, when we had our formal launch in June. The advertising was effective, and the number of customers kept growing. That was how we got our first ten customers. We repeated this process to get our next 100 customers, and our next 1000 customers after that.

I encourage the entrepreneurs I work with, especially the early stage ones, not to worry about developing a scalable sales process. Just get to ten customers any way you can.

I've been amazed at the clever approaches I've seen the entrepreneurs that I've worked with take to get their first ten customers. Here are three clever approaches and one obvious approach:

A. Meetups.

"James" went to meet ups of other entrepreneurs in his metro area. He would give a pitch about what his company did.

The pitches led to conversations that would lead to

customers. James built his revenue from $0 to over $1 million using this technique.

A variance of this technique is:

B. Facebook groups.

"Aric" found his first customers through Facebook groups. Aric's strategy was pretty simple.

Aric would communicate with other businesses in a group. He would provide value, by providing his insights for free. Once he showed his expertise, some of these businesses would convert into customers.

Obviously, this is not a repeatable process. However, it is a great way to grow your initial revenue and get your business growing.

You could also enlist:

C. Brokers.

That's what "Andrew" did.

This is one I would never have thought would work in a million years. However, it was very successful. It was because the brokers in Andrew's space were an untapped sales channel that had a huge incentive to actually sell Andrew's product.

The broker network has grown Andrew's business to close to $10 million/year.

D. Your network.

I'm saving the most obvious one for last, because there seems to be a stigma entrepreneurs have against tapping their network for customers. However, you should absolutely use your network when you're starting out.

It should be obvious, but your network will be happy to help you. All you have to do is ask. Nevertheless, I always see entrepreneurs unwilling to use their networks.

Asking for help from people you know, gives you the best chance of success. You get the stamp of approval from someone who has credibility. That helps a lot.

How Do You Win Really Big Deals?

The biggest one shot deal I ever won was a $25 million/year custom deal we did with Lucent.

We had been doing business with Lucent's optical module division in the UK and Pennsylvania for years. In fact, we were getting all of their business.

However, we couldn't crack Lucent's box business. We had significantly better products than our competitors, but we just kept losing.

Lucent then issued a Request For Quote (RFQ) for a custom device. They wanted the custom product in three months!

It was unheard of in the world of Analog semiconductors. However, I knew we could do it. I was tired of losing. I decided we were going to give them exactly what they wanted, at the exact schedule we wanted.

However, meeting Lucent's exact schedule created a set of hurdles we had to overcome.

Hurdle number one: Convincing the engineering

team we could actually meet Lucent's request.

You can imagine the pushback I got. It went like this, "Three months! There's no way we can do this!"

There actually were the requisite expletives thrown in. Since I'm trying to eliminate expletives from my writing, I'll let your imagination figure out what they were.

I pointed out that we actually had many of the components Lucent wanted. All we needed to do was combine them together into one IC. Yes, there would be considerable non-trivial engineering work, but we could do it, if we managed the schedule on a daily basis.

More expletives flew from the engineering director's mouth. I think he said I was a lunatic at one point.

I suggested we work through the engineering schedule together.

The engineering director calmed down enough to go through the work with me. That is when he understood it was ridiculously difficult, but possible. This leads to...

Hurdle number two: Managing the engineering project.

The engineering director correctly pointed out, "What if we fail and don't meet the schedule."

My answer was simple. "Then it's on me. I'll take the blame. However, we're not going to fail. We're going to manage every engineer involved in the project on a daily basis."

The engineering director was bought in, sort of. We needed to find a project manager to oversee the whole project and run the daily engineering meeting that we would need to have.

We both thought Doug would be the right person to manage the project. We would have two teams (one in Portland, Oregon and the other in Germany) develop the chip.

Now that I had the agreement of the engineering team, I went back to Lucent and presented our bid. It was an aggressive schedule with an aggressive price to boot.

A week later, Lucent told us we had won the bid! The hard work would now begin.

Doug did an awesome job managing the project. We developed a daily progress schedule for each engineer involved in the project.

We knew if an engineer was ahead or behind schedule on the project. The daily meeting Doug ran focused on helping any engineers that were behind schedule.

It worked.

Three months later, we hand delivered the working product to Lucent on the exact day we promised.

The moral of the story: Don't let someone tell you something can't be done.

We won $25 million/year of business because we didn't just mail in an easy answer. We pushed and took the customer's perspective.

The customer wanted the product in three months. There was a way to get there. That's how you win business.

What Can You Learn from A Little Boy and A LEGO?

I was at home Saturday night enjoying a really nice evening with my wife and daughter. We had just finished dinner, and I was thumbing through one of my Twitter feeds.

That's when I saw this tweet:

Boy writes to Lego, after losing a minifigure.

Lego's customer service department should run the world.

I clicked on the response and I was blown away!

Wow!

Whatever LEGO is doing must be good. Not just good, but incredibly good because LEGO is encouraging its customer support people to break the rules to satisfy customers.

LEGO is saying, "Screw the rules. Don't worry about how much money it's going to cost. Just make the customer happy."

The great news is you can take this customer centric approach with your business today. It doesn't matter if you are just a one-person company, you can do this today!

Just follow the story of the boy and the LEGO.

When you see what Richard, the LEGO customer support person, did, you'll be blown away too!

Here's the story of what happened to Luka, the boy that lost his Lego mini-figure in Luka's words:

"Hello. My name is Luka. I am seven years old. With all the money I got for Christmas, I bought the Ninjago kit of the Utrasonic Raider. The number is 9449. My Daddy took me to Sainsburys and told me to leave the people at home but I took them and I lost Jay ZX at the shop as it fell out of my coat. I am really upset I have lost him. Daddy said to send to you an email to see if you will send me another one. I promise I won't take him to the shop if you can. Thank you."

Richard's response is a textbook example of why empowering your people and throwing away the call center scripts is the best way to go.

Let's analyze Richard's response to his customer, Luka, and see how you can use this as a framework for your own customer service organization.

Paragraph 1:

"We are sorry to hear about you losing your Jay minifigure, but it sounds like your dad might have been right about leaving it at home. It sounds like you are very sad about it too."

Richard does a really nice job of acknowledging Luka's request. He does two really smart things to build rapport with his customer:

He acknowledges that Luka's Dad might have been right about keeping the figure at home.

He acknowledges that Luka is sad about losing the mini-figure.

Paragraph 2:

"Normally we would ask you to pay for a new one, if you lose one of your mini-figures and need to have it replaced. My bosses told me I could not send you one for free because you lost it, but I decided I would put a call into Sensei Wu to see if he could help me."

This is absolutely brilliant! Richard is using the LEGO language and talking kid to kid about how Sensei Wu (another Lego character) can help. Therefore, Richard is continuing to promote the LEGO brand AND help Luka. He's also telling Luka he's doing something special for him that he normally shouldn't do.

Paragraph 3:

"Luka I told Sensei Wu that losing your Jay mini-figure was purely an accident and you would never ever ever let it happen again. He told me to tell you, "Luka, your father seems like a very wise man. You must always protect your Ninjago mini-figures like the dragons protect the Weapons of Spinjitzu!" Sensei Wu also told me that it was okay if I sent you a new Jay and told me it would be okay if I included something extra for you, because anyone that saves their Christmas money to buy the Ultransonic Raider must be a really big Ninjago fan."

Imagine the smile on Luka's face, when he read paragraph 3! He was probably running around his house telling his Dad the exciting news!

If Luka wasn't a customer for life, he is now! Think about the economics for just a second. Richard spent maybe $10 (and I'm being generous) of the Lego's money to make Luka happy.

How much money will Luka spend on LEGOs for the rest his life?

How much money will Luka's children spend on LEGOs for the rest of their lives?

How many friends will Luka tell about his amazing experience with Lego customer service?

How much will they buy?

LEGO customer support, because of Richard's actions just hit a grand slam home run for Lego!

Paragraph 4:

"So I hope you enjoy your Jay minifigure with all his

weapons. You actually have the only Jay minifigure that combines 3 different Jays into one! I am also going to send you a bad guy for him to fight!"

Luka now knows he's getting the extra bonus (the bad guy for Jay to fight). How cool is that?

Paragraph 5 & 6:

"Just remember what Sensei Wu said: keep your minifigures protected like the Weapons of Spinjitzu! And of course, always listen to your dad.

"Luka you will see an envelope from LEGO within the next two weeks with your new minifigures. Please take good care of them, Luka. Remember that you promised to always leave them at home.

"Happy Building!

"Sincerely,

"Richard

"LEGO Consumer Services"

Richard again stays in the character of his company. He tells Luka when to expect the new minifigures. I'll bet Luka ran to the mailbox every day to see if there was a package from LEGO.

Not every business is LEGO. You probably don't have Sensei Wu to help you out.

However, you do have real live human beings communicating with other real live human beings. You might also be just starting out, and you are the customer service organization (along with everything else).

The key to a great customer experience, is using your common sense and forgetting the rules.

Imagine if Richard had said, "Sorry, there's nothing we can do to help you."

Luka would have been really sad. Maybe he would have learned the lesson never to take his minifigures out of the house. However, he would not love LEGO the way he surely does now.

Steve Jobs always talked about being insanely great. Insanely great applies not just to the physical product or service you are selling. Being insanely great is about the whole experience of doing business with your company.

Any time you touch the customer, is another chance to make the experience insanely great.

Think about your website. Is the customer experience pleasant and easy to navigate, or is it painful?

Think about your sales process. Is the sales process easy or difficult?

Think about your technical support. Is your support team trained to be like LEGO's?

Think about when someone picks up the telephone and calls you. How does your administrative team represent your brand?

Think about when someone emails you. Do you promptly get the person an answer or do they go into a black hole?

Every interaction with your customers is a chance for you to make the customer experience insanely great. It is just like Luka's experience with LEGO.

Train your team to break the rules, like Richard at LEGO did.

Do it today.

Watch all the great things that happen.

How You Can Avoid Nine
Startup Sales Killers

"I t's too early to hire a VP of Sales!" The VC said to me. "You should be doing the selling!"

"I hear where you're coming from," I said. "And believe me, I will be selling.

"'Ken's' been part of the company, since I started it.

"Without Ken, we wouldn't have gotten funded," I said. "One of our investors insisted we have the sales piece figured out."

It turned out we were both right.

I did need Ken to start the company. I don't think we would have been funded without him.

However, the VC was also right. It was WAY too early to have a VP of Sales.

I was the most effective salesperson the company at the start. The company was my idea, and I was passionate about what we were doing in a way that Ken never could be. I'll get back to this later.

- Do the selling yourself when you are starting out. You'll be...

- The most effective salesperson your company has because you know the product(s) the best, and...

- You, the CEO, will care the most about winning deals because it's your company, and...

- You'll learn the sales process for your company, so you'll know what to look for when you eventually hire a true VP of Sales.

I wish the list of mistakes you can make with sales ended with hiring a VP of Sales too early. There are many more mistakes you can make with startup sales.

Here's a list of 8 other mistakes to avoid:

A. Don't hire a B player for VP of Sales, because this is the best person you can find

I made this mistake too.

Ken didn't work out, because he didn't want to put out the effort required. He was burned out from too many years on the road. Therefore, I hired an Executive Recruiter (the right move) to help me find a replacement.

I looked at hundreds of resumes and interviewed around twenty candidates. None of the candidates were what I called, "Wows."

A Wow candidate is someone that blows you away on every metric you are looking for. We just couldn't find a Wow candidate.

The reality is we were just too early to attract a Wow VP of Sales candidate. We needed more traction to attract the Wows.

We just weren't there yet.

However, there were two candidates who stood out from the rest. Both candidates were good solid "B" players.

What should I have done? It is easy. I should have passed on both candidates and kept running sales, until we got to a level where we could attract a Wow VP of Sales.

I ended up hiring one of the candidates. He did some good things for the company, but he wasn't at the level we wanted.

The moral of the story is hire only Wow people.

B. While you are interviewing, you shouldn't hire based just on personality.

Sales can be considered a squishy thing. The reality is that today's successful VP of Sales is metric and systems based, not just a people person.

Here are some questions that any qualified VP of Sales should be able to answer:

"What type of people you want to bring with you to our company?"

A good VP of Sales (just about any executive for that matter) has some people that they would like to bring with them.

You don't need to know the names of the people. However, a good VP of Sales should be able to tell you about the people and what roles they will fill.

"How will the sales organization look in 90 days, based on what you know?"

A qualified VP of Sales will be able to tell you how they feel the sales organization will evolve.

They should have a definitive step-by-step plan.

"How did you build your current sales organization?"

A qualified VP of Sales should be able to tell you how they built their current organization.

In fact, they should be able to tell you how they've built every organization they've managed. It's a red flag, if they can't tell you.

"What is the biggest deal that you've won and how did you win it?"

You're again looking for details here. The more precise the candidate is, the better.

"What is the biggest deal you've lost and why did you lose it?"

No one wins every deal. A good VP of Sales should have no problems telling you about their losses and what they would do different.

Remember, you're looking for methodology, process and detail.

Let's say you've hired a VP of Sales that isn't working out.

C. Don't keep a weak VP of Sales, once you realize you've made a mistake.

We all make hiring mistakes. Hiring a VP of Sales who doesn't work out is common.

What you do next can determine if your company survives. You need to terminate the VP of Sales who isn't working out, as soon as you see it.

How quickly can you see if a VP of Sales is working out? The answer is as fast as your sales cycle is.

Let's say your sales cycle (the amount of time it takes from a lead being captured to a lead turning into a customer) is six months. You should know by the end of that six-month period, if your new VP of Sales is working out.

Here's the mistake too many people make: They hope things will get better.

The problem is you're burning through time while you wait. Time is the enemy when you're building a company.

Let's say you've hired an awesome VP of Sales. Don't screw it up by...

D. Don't screw it up by setting the initial revenue targets for your VP of Sales.

I know it's tempting, but don't do it. You want your new VP of Sales to own the numbers.

Even if the numbers are low, let the new VP of Sales set the initial numbers. You can step in later, if the VP of Sales isn't aggressive enough.

Okay. How else can you screw up sales?

E. Don't think you have a repeatable sales process, when you don't.

What happens when you get that first big win? Maybe it's not even a big win, but a medium sized win.

It's human nature to believe the floodgates have opened, and you now have a repeatable sales process. You probably don't.

What does a repeatable sales model mean? It is exactly that, something that is consistent.

A repeatable sales model doesn't mean that sales have grown 30% for one month. That's just not enough data.

A repeatable sales model does mean that sales have grown 30% month on month for the past six months. You also have a set of predictable actions that have led to the outcome.

However, maybe things aren't going as planned.

F. You can make it worse by hiring for growth that doesn't happen.

This is a classic mistake.

You get a couple of wins, then you start feeling good about yourself. You then hire a large sales team and a staff to support them.

You find that sales slow down and you end up lay-ing-off the same team you just hired. tI is a huge morale killer.

 You can make it worse.

G. As tempting as it may be, don't pay for leads.

Of all the scammy, crazy ways to blow money, pay-ing for leads has to be right near the top of the list.

It's kind of like what Pied Piper did near the end of Season 3 of Silicon Valley to show user growth.

Paying for leads just never, ever works out. It is be-cause the quality of the leads usually sucks.

Think about it. Why is someone going to give you

high quality leads, instead of using the leads themselves? It just doesn't make sense.

Hopefully, you don't succumb to buying leads.

H. You shouldn't farm out a portion of your sales activity to an outside consultant.

Let me explain.

Let's say there's a group of people that, allegedly, have extensive contacts in a region where you have no presence. The group comes highly recommended.

You meet with the group several times. You are impressed with the group's knowledge and hire them on a monthly retainer.

You find that the group does nothing, except take your money.

That's where the alarm bells should go off. Never pay outside sales reps (which is what a group like this is) a retainer.

The commission you are giving them, should be enough of an incentive. Pass, if it isn't enough.

There you have it. This is my list of nine startup sales mistakes that you should never make.

There are many more sales mistakes you can make. However, you'll be doing good if you avoid this set of nine sales mistakes.

5 Avoidable Marketing Mistakes That Can Kill Your Startup

L et me ask you a question. If you had a machine where you could put in money and for every dollar you put in you got two dollars back, wouldn't you be stuffing money into that machine as fast as you could?

If you do marketing right, it is a cash machine for you. What should your marketing spend be, if it is a positive return?

You should spend as much as humanly possible. You can't spend enough money on marketing, if the return is positive.

Unfortunately, many aspiring CEOs don't understand the power of marketing.

Years ago, I had the following conversation with a new General Manager. He eventually became CEO of the company we were working at:

"I don't understand why we need to spend money on marketing our products," the General Manager said to me. "We have all these salespeople. Don't they know everything that's going on?"

I was stunned by his answer, but I wasn't surprised. The General Manager was new to the job.

The General Manager was previously an engineering manager with no previous customer experience. He just assumed that salespeople know everything going on with any given customer.

This conversation happened almost twenty years ago. Things have only gotten more difficult for salespeople in subsequent years.

You have to build a relationship with your customers. That is where the successful use of marketing comes in.

Unfortunately, I've seen many marketing mistakes that startup CEOs have made during the last few years. The good news is these mistakes are easy to identify and fix, so let me get going.

Marketing Mistake Number One: Not having a plan.

Not having a plan, if you can believe it, happens very often. How do you win, if you don't have a plan?

It's the old "Build it and they will come model." Customers somehow are just going to find you.

I was just talking to a CEO a couple of months ago. The CEO was wondering why his business wasn't growing.

"How do customers find you?" I asked.

"Through our website," he said.

"What are you doing to drive traffic to your website?"

There was a long pause. It was clear that he didn't have a plan.

What did he need to do? Have a plan!

You can't just expect customers to find your website. Those days are long gone.

You have to figure out how your customers are going to find you. You are also going to have to figure out how you're going to nurture these opportunities into leads for your business.

Marketing Mistake Number Two: Jumping from plan to plan.

Jumping from plan to plan is almost as bad as not having a plan. It may actually be worse, because you're likely spending (wasting) money.

You see CEOs jump from plan to plan, if they have never done marketing before. For example, I was advising a CEO on his marketing strategy.

The CEO had developed a plan to run ads on Facebook. The ads ran for a couple of days and then stopped running.

I asked the CEO what happened to the ads. He said, "The ads aren't converting, so I decided to run ads on Google."

You have to give your advertising plans a long time, before they will pay off. Two days is just not enough time. You're just getting started.

You have to plan on a lot longer time, if you expect your marketing plans to pay off. When you jump from plan to plan, it is a recipe for disaster.

You should test your marketing first, and then build out your strategy, based on your testing. The testing is likely to take at least one month if not longer, depending upon the marketing you're doing.

The thing about marketing is that it has an iterative effect. You need to be consistent with your marketing. I saw this iterative effect with my last company.

We were consistent with our marketing. Each marketing campaign built on the success of the previous campaign.

The results were okay to begin with and kept improving with time.

That is what you need to do. You need to market week after week and month after month. Marketing builds on itself. The more you market, the better the results you are going to get.

Moving from plan to plan will make you look

schizophrenic and will not work. Your marketing plan is like a good wine. It needs time to breathe.

Marketing Mistake Number Three: Having too many marketing channels at once.

Instead of just focusing on Facebook, you've decided to focus on Google. "Oh yeah, let's go add in some print advertising. We've got a lot of money to spend, so let's go spend money on radio and TV advertising too." You get the idea.

It is a huge mistake when you are starting your business to focus on multiple channels at once. Start with one channel and get it to work.

When you master that one channel, then you move on to a second channel. When you master the second channel, and you think, "maybe I can increase the audience by including a third channel?" You can then move on to a third channel.

You should do your marketing in this stair-step approach of one channel at a time. You're going to find that mastering that one channel is going to be difficult enough.

Marketing Mistake Number Four: Not measuring your results.

It is criminal in today's world, with all the digital tools we have available, not to measure your marketing results. You should be measuring everything you can think of.

- Return on investment, which you should always be measuring

- Cost per click

- Cost per action

- Cost per lead

You can measure all of it. The beautiful thing about measuring your results, is you have benchmarks.

You now know whether you are improving or declining. You can see whether you are improving.

There is no more guesswork, like there was for me back in the day.

Marketing Mistake Number Five: You're not spending enough money on marketing.

Let me ask you another question. You're getting a return of $2 for every $1 you are investing in your marketing program. However, you are limiting your marketing budget.

You're measuring your results, so you know exactly what your return on investment is. You have a plan. You're using the stair-step strategy, so you're not jumping from strategy to strategy.

The question is why aren't you spending more money? Seriously, what's stopping you?

What Are Three Ways You Can Lose Your Customers?

"I'd like a tall decaf and a jade citrus mint tea," I said. The coffee is for me, and the tea is for Blossom.

"I'm sorry, but we're out of filters. Will an americano be okay instead?"

"Yes, it will," I answered.

I see the barista is ringing me up at $2.65. That is the price of an americano, instead of the $2.15 I would be paying for a tall coffee.

I looked at the barista and said, "I'm okay with the americano, but you should charge me at the tall decaf price. After all, you're out of the filters."

"I'm sorry sir, but I'll get in trouble if I do that," was the response.

"Really? You're out of the filters after all."

She stood firm and repeated, "I'm sorry sir. I will get in trouble if I do that."

"I understand," I said. "Is your manager around?"

"I'm the supervisor," she said proudly. "The manager isn't due back for an hour."

I smiled and let her ring me up.

$0.50 seems like a small amount. Certainly, for Starbucks, the $0.50 isn't going to change their fortunes, and it definitely wasn't going to change my fortunes.

However, I have to admit that I was pissed. Starbucks has already made ordering decaf an ordeal at many stores. Getting charged more for their mistake, was close to the final straw.

You lose customers, when you don't put your customers first.

You have to ask yourself, if you're willing to lose customers over $0.50.

The day before I was meeting with my good friend and business partner, Cathal, for coffee over at Peets. I asked for a small decaf coffee.

"We're out right now," the barista said to me. However, I'm not worried because I know what I'm going to hear next.

"We'll have to brew a new batch," the barista said. "It will take a few minutes. Will that be okay?" He asked.

"That will be fine," I say. I vow that I will give Peets

as much of my business as possible going forward.

It's so easy. Just put your customers first. It's such a powerful differentiator.

Here are three other ways you can lose customers:

A. Your product quality is poor.

Years ago, I was meeting with executives from Hitachi. Hitachi was one of the biggest customers we had for my business unit.

We exchanged pleasantries, and then one of the executives started talking. Watanabe, our Japan country manager, translated for me.

I could hear by their tone, that they were pissed.

"They are saying there's a problem with the product. They are also saying that you should know what the problem is."

"We've never had a problem with that product. Can you tell them that we will figure out what the issue is immediately?" I was trying to make things right.

The executives didn't wait for Watanabe to translate. They produced photos showing how the product was misbehaving. The executive then started talking again in Japanese.

"They say you should know there is a problem," Watanabe said again.

I was a little frustrated. I asked Watanabe, "What

am I supposed to say? They may have uncovered something that our testing missed.

"Let them know that we are embarrassed by the lapse in our quality, and we will take full responsibility to fix it."

The executives again didn't wait for the translation. This time though, they stood up and walked out of the meeting room.

It was the first and only time I'd ever had that happen in my career. I don't think we lost Hitachi as a customer, because they had no choice but to use our product.

However, I also had no doubt that that they weren't going to give us any business, unless they absolutely had to.

B. You don't test your product.

I was on the other end of this beauty as a customer, when I was doing board level design. I was buying a chip that there was only one source for. The chip wasn't working right, because the temperature on our board increased.

It made no sense what was going on. The problem had shut our production line down. That's a killer.

I called the company we were buying the chip from, and they told me something chilling, "We don't temperature test our products."

"Your data sheet guarantees your product will work over temperature. What am I supposed to do?"

I eventually spoke with the head of the product line. They agreed to test the product for us.

Can you imagine that? I was relieved that they would test the product for us, but the damage was done. I again vowed that I would never buy anything from them again.

C. You don't ship your product, when you committed to.

Anyone that was a customer of my old company, Maxim Integrated Products, knows that Maxim had a history, to say it nicely, of missing deliveries. When I say we missed deliveries at Maxim, I don't mean by just a day. We could literally be weeks or months late.

It was our Achilles heel as a company. The crazy thing was, we did it by design.

Maxim's CEO, the late Jack Gifford, was absolutely paranoid about holding excess inventory. He also believed that customers would forgive us for our sins.

Well, he was sort of right. Some of the smaller customers did forgive us for our sins, because our products were really good.

However, there were many customers who banned

their engineers from using our products. It wasn't until we started doing large amounts of business with Apple and Samsung that the problem got fixed.

ROUND 10: WHAT ARE YOU GONNA DO, WHEN YOU GET PUNCHED IN THE MOUTH?

What If Facebook Enters Your Market?

"**W**elcome."

That was Steve Jobs' famous response, when IBM entered the PC market in 1981. Maybe Jobs should have been more worried.

After all, by 1984 IBM sold $4 billion worth of PCs, compared to Apple's $2 billion.

The question of "What if Facebook/Google/IBM/ Texas Instruments/Intel/ (name your tech behemoth here) enters your market?" has been around forever. It's a favorite question for investors to ask, when you're raising money.

It is not as if investors don't know the answer. They do know the answer. What investors want to see, is your reaction to the question.

Investors already know that almost nothing (except bulletproof patent protection, and that's rare) stops any company in any industry from implementing the same new feature/product/service that you just implemented. They also know that small companies (startups) have many advantages, versus their larger competitors.

I used to get asked a variation of this question (in my case it was, "What if Texas Instruments or Maxim or Analog Devices or Linear Technology come after you?"), when I was raising money. The answer was always the same.

"Nothing is going to stop them. It will take their best people to do what we are doing.

"However, we have a huge advantage versus them: our lives depend on it. To them, this is just another product line. We are going to fight and kick the shit out of them. Here's how we will do it…"

That is exactly what happened. We were focused and we executed at a really high level. We cared about every potential deal. Our established competition cared, but at nowhere near the same level that we did.

It's a mistake to believe that your competitors don't have great people.

Your competitors do have great people. Sometimes, they may even have better people than you do. When you are thinking about what market to enter, you need to be strategic because:

Market Choice Is Everything!

Choose a market that is right in your competitor's sweet spot (something they really care deeply about), and it will be difficult to win. It will not be impossible, but very difficult. You'll need game changing technology, and, even then, you might not win.

Choose a market that's not core to your competitors and you have a better chance. Yes, it might not be as sexy as beating Apple in the iPhone market, but you can still win and win big.

I'll never forget years ago, when I was an EIR (Entrepreneur in Residence) for a VC firm located in San Francisco. It was Monday, which was the day that companies would present to the whole partnership.

On this particular Monday, a very charismatic CEO with a great pedigree was pitching the partnership. His company had invented a better product aimed right at the heart of a major semiconductor company's business.

Everyone was impressed.

It looked like the firm was going to invest. (I'll get back to this later.)

I've Seen Both Scenarios Happen.

The interesting thing to me is that I saw this play out early in my career, when I was with the young upstart company (Maxim) attacking the established companies (National Semiconductor, Analog Devices, and Texas Instruments). We cared more than the other guys did and we won.

The way to defeat the larger competitor, is to not let them gain any headway in your market. They'll then go back to focusing on what they do best.

However, as Maxim grew in size, the company started entering new markets dominated by smaller, nimbler competitors. For example, I was running a division of Maxim that was focused on the communications space during the late 1990's.

Our chief competitors were AMCC and Vitesse, but Analog Devices (a larger company than we were) also had a small product offering. I'll never forget telling our CEO, the late Jack Gifford, that I was really worried about Analog Devices, but I thought we would destroy AMCC and Vitesse. Jack nodded his head in agreement.

I got it completely backwards.

Analog Devices never became the threat that I expected them to be. We had superior products than AMCC and Vitesse and we offered our products at a lower price. However, we couldn't unseat them.

Why?

Communications was the only business that AMCC and Vitesse had. They fought like their lives depended upon it (because their lives did depend upon it). It was just another product line to us.

Don't underestimate the power of focus!

Small companies have a massive advantage versus big company. The small company is laser-focused on one goal. The big company will inevitably be focused on many goals.

Small companies usually move super-quickly, because they are not bogged down with politics. Big companies, where many senior and mid-level managers are primarily concerned with protecting their turf, tend to move at a much slower pace.

Remember the 80/20 Rule.

You can almost be guaranteed that 80% of LargeCo's revenue is coming from one of its five divisions. Where do you think the centralized sales organization is going to focus to meet its goals?

That's right: on the 80%.

This is where the opportunity is for your startup. You can focus on the soft underbelly and win. You're 110% focused on your area, and they are not.

You can attack other, larger market segments next. You earn the right to do this, after you've dominated the smaller market segments.

Can you win going after the largest segment of the market?

Sure, you can. However, this takes much better

execution. You're going to have to be significantly better than your competitors and you're going to need a huge amount of luck.

You will also need luck going after the soft underbelly. However, much less will be required.

Success in business is hard enough, so my recommendation is to make things as easy as possible for yourself.

What happened with the VC firm's investment with the charismatic CEO?

I was also impressed with the CEO. The guy really knew what he was doing. However, I had a concern I raised to the partners:

"He's trying to steal their (his competitor's) lunch. He's targeting 80% of their existing business, and they are going to throw all their resources against him to prevent it." I recommended that we pass on the investment.

I was shouted down.

The firm made the investment, and $100 million and several years later, the company was liquidated for pennies on the dollar.

Oops.

What Are the Five Fatal Mistakes That Will Kill Your Business?

D id you know that it took me three founding teams, before I was able to get the right team to start my company? It's true.

Team number one failed, because my two co-founders quit and stole the intellectual property of the company. They left me for dead, the day before we were going to get funded.

Team number two failed, because the team wasn't strong enough.

Team number three succeeded, because we had the right combination of people with the same vision and meshed well as a team. Nevertheless, two of the five founders were out of the company within one year of receiving funding.

Is it any wonder why most startups fail?

What are the numbers? Depending upon the survey you read, approximately 70% of all startups fail.

Do you want to be another one of the startups that fail?

Good. I didn't think so.

Here's my list of some obvious and some, maybe, not so obvious reasons that startups fail. The good news is you can recover from many of these mistakes or problems. Let's get started:

A. You have the wrong team.

As I pointed out, I went through two teams before I got to the right team. However, I was lucky.

You may not be so lucky. Here's the most important advice I can give you:

Don't settle, especially with founders.

You need everything to be right between yourself and your co-founders, if you are going to succeed. This doesn't mean you can't have differences. It does mean that you need to have mutual respect.

You're going to want your co-founders to have integrity, be smart and passionate about the company and be cultural fits for the company. The tough part is that some, if not all, of these traits may not be obvious when you bring on a co-founder.

That's why some co-founders leave a company early. It's natural and normal to have a co-founder leave. You just need to protect yourself and the company.

B. Your company culture's not right.

Maybe I should have started with company culture, because you need to be thinking about your company culture, before you bring on your first co-founder.

A commitment culture, where your team is truly committed to the company, is the culture that gives you the most chance of success. The commitment culture starts with you.

You need to foster this inclusive culture every step of the way. Every new person you add to the company either reinforces or hurts your commitment culture. That is why you want to be very careful with who you bring into the company.

C. You don't have a go to market strategy, or your go to market strategy is poorly thought out.

It's not enough to have a great product. The days of "build it and they will come" are long gone.

Having a website is not enough. Having a sales force is not enough. It is also not enough to say that you are going to advertise.

You really need to think about how your customers are going to find you. You will them need to figure out how much it's going to cost you. The best book I've read on the subject is Traction: How Any Startup Can Achieve Explosive Growth by Gabriel Weinberg. Traction gives you a systematic process to figure out what marketing channels will work for you.

D. Financials? What financials?

Be honest. How many of you don't really know how much money you are making or losing?

I've seen the lack of a financial plan or a poorly constructed financial plan bite many startups. Here are some basics to think about.

Are you paying yourself a salary? You should be, even if it's a small amount. You don't want to just take money out of the company, when you need it.

You should know EXACTLY how much money you are spending every month. You should know EXACTLY how much money your product costs to make.

You should know when (what year and what month) your company will hit cash-flow break-even. You should set the revenue level at cash-flow break-even.

Develop a financial plan today if you haven't done so already. It doesn't have to be complex.

What is the one mistake that's almost 100% guaranteed to kill your company?

E. Investor/Company Mismatch.

The one absolutely, nearly 100% guaranteed company killer is a bad investor.

For example, what if 50% of Apple shareholders wanted the company to sell?

What is you received a loan from your parents to start your company? All of a sudden, your father wanted his money back.

What if one of your investors can no longer support the company and it leaves you with no money left to operate?

How do you recover, if you are in any of these situations? The answer is you usually don't.

Therefore, choose your investors wisely.

Make sure your family understands up front how long it's going to take for you to pay them back, if you take money from your family. You should be honest because it will probably take several years.

Make sure your vision for the company is the same as your investor, if you take money from an Angel or VC. You should pay close attention to how you are being treated during the fundraising process.

Do your diligence on your investors. Talk to other people that have taken money from them. Did the investors hang in for the long run or did the investors cut bait at the first sign of trouble?

Most importantly of all, get a lawyer! Even if you are taking money from your family, you should get a good, knowledgeable lawyer to draft (or evaluate) the agreement, so it is fair. I know getting a lawyer can be expensive, but this will be money well spent.

There are things you just don't know as a first-time entrepreneur.

Some of these errors can make it very difficult to succeed. You can overcome team issues, culture issues, go to market issues and the lack of financial discipline. However, a lack of investor support, whether it is your family or more traditional investors, can you make it next to impossible for you to succeed.

What Should You Do To Save Your Business When It Falters?

"It's even worse than I thought it would be," I told Steve. "Everything is completely broken. Revenue is cratering. Product quality is horrible. The strategy sucks. I think the team needs be completely replaced.

"Besides that, everything's great," I laughed.

I had taken over one of three divisions that the company had three months earlier. I spent the previous three months assessing what needed to be fixed.

I knew going in that there would be problems. However, I never thought there were going to be so many problems.

You can feel like you're overwhelmed, when your business is faltering.

It can feel like you don't know where to start, when your business starts dropping. I've been there, so I know what you're going through.

You can follow the same four-step process I followed, when the business I was running was dropping. However, I'm going to start with an important pre-step you can take BEFORE your business happens to drop:

Pre Step: Develop A Worst Case Plan

Far too few people develop a downside plan, but you shouldn't be one of them. You're clear headed, when your business is going well. Now is a great time think about the what ifs. Here are some that you should be actively thinking about:

What if you're revenue suddenly drops?

What if the competition suddenly drops prices by 30%? How will you respond?

What if your costs suddenly shoot up?

What if your key marketing channel stops working?

What if your key manufacturing partner goes out of business?

What if your accounts receivables suddenly shoot up by $16 million?

I've seen all of these things happen during my business career. The smart thing to do is to develop contingencies.

Some of the contingencies are logistical, such as always having two manufacturers for any product you build. Other contingencies are of the planning variety, such as developing a worst-case financial plan.

You may or may not be able to figure out all the possible contingencies, but you can definitely develop a worst-case financial plan.

A worst-case plan is critical, especially for bootstrapped startups, because you can't to afford to run out of money. It's not hard to do.

At least you will have a financial plan that you can follow, just in case things go bad. You can refer back to that plan that you developed, just in case the bottom falls out of your business.

Let's talk about the four-step plan that I referred to above. about the focus is on what to do, when your business is failing. I will present these steps in a serial fashion. However, the reality is you that may do one or all four steps at the same time.

Many of these steps are really painful to take. Think of this process as being similar to having to amputate a limb to save the body. Okay, here we go.

Step 1: Where Are You Losing Business?

This first step is the beginning of peeling the onion, on where your problem is. Here are the things to look for:

If you have a business focused on a few customers, then it should be pretty easy to figure out which customer isn't buying anymore. However, if you're not so lucky, then you'll have to look a little harder.

You can look at:

A. Geography.

Check your numbers by region, to see if a certain region has dropped off. For example, years ago, a business I was running dominated the Japanese market.

Our business then dropped off in Japan. We, therefore, knew where we needed to investigate for possible reasons. This leads me to the next possible cause:

B. Marketing channel.

Sometimes one issue can lead you to another issue. You need to look at your marketing channels, as part of your initial analysis.

In the case of the business we were losing in Japan, it turned out that we were losing business at one particular distributor, out of the three major Japanese distributors we had. It turned out to be a pretty wild story that I will get back to in a bit.

Now that you've figured out where you are losing business, here is the next step:

Step 2: Why Are You Losing Business?

The detective work now begins.

The following are some possibilities from my experience of turning businesses around.

A. The end market for your product has suddenly

stopped buying.

I've lived this nightmare during the communications bubble. That was one of the many problems I inherited at the company I joined years ago. It was ugly. The whole market stopped buying at the same time.

B. A competitor entered the market and is eating your lunch.

Sometimes you can get complacent, because of your success. It's a competitive world out there. If you're successful, someone is likely trying to find a way to knock you down.

Make sure that you are always reviewing what your competitors are doing. You should also be taking the pulse of your customers. If you are losing business, you need to know who you're losing business to.

C. The market needs have changed, and you didn't notice.

Markets are dynamic. Sometimes the market needs can be slowly changing, without your business taking a hit. However, suddenly your business will then drop.

That's why, as I said above, you need to monitor what your competitors are doing. You also need to understand how the dynamics of your specific market are changing.

D. The quality of your product has changed.

Product quality is a big issue for manufacturers of physical products. Maybe you changed suppliers, and, even though your product is passing your quality tests, it is failing in the field.

The good news is that many times your angry customers will tell you about your problems.

E. Your marketing channel isn't working the way it once did.

This is a very common problem, especially if you're using a social media channel, like Facebook, to promote your products. The algorithms are constantly changing, so you have to continually monitor the ROI on your marketing.

It could also be what we faced in Japan, where one of our distributors was marking up the prices on our products by three times what they should have. We caught the mistake, because someone that worked for me had studied in Japan during high school and read Japanese script.

F. A major customer stopped buying.

Your revenue is a perfect place to start, especially if you have a few customers that dominate your revenue. In fact, going back to the pre-planning concept I spoke about earlier, always have a contingency plan, if you have revenue concentration.

Too many businesses have died because one large customer stopped buying or reduced their buying. You don't want to be one of them.

Now that you've identified where and why you're losing business, it's time to...

Step 3: Stop the Bleeding, By Narrowing Your Focus And Doubling Down.

I will not say that every turnaround, but over 90% of them involve narrowing your focus. The narrowing can take many different forms including:

A. Narrowing your marketing channels

There's a part of your marketing that's working and there's a part of your marketing that isn't working. Eliminate the part that isn't working and double down on the part that is.

Let's say that Facebook advertising is failing, but your AdWords ROI is positive. The solution is obvious: Double down on AdWords.

B. Narrowing your customer focus

You've lost your big customers, but your small customers are growing or vice-versa. The solution is obvious: Stop trying to get the big customers and double down on growing your small customer business.

C. Narrowing your product focus

Trying to be all things to all people, is a classic mistake that happens frequently. You start out your business growing in market A. Then you decide you'd like to be in markets B, C, and D.

You are doing okay but not great in these new markets, until the bottom falls out. Your strategy is simply to get out of businesses B, C, and D and double down on business A.

Step 4: Come Back Stronger

Now that you've narrowed your focus, and you've doubled down on your core competencies, you're ready to come back stronger. There is one more painful step left to take.

You are likely going to have let some people go. This is the hardest part of turning a business around.

Make no mistake that the people you are letting go have done nothing wrong. They were just doing their jobs.

You did something wrong, by making the bad investments in the wrong places. Someone else will now likely have to pay for your mistakes with their job.

You should have some humility, as you undertake the changes you are about to make.

How Your Startup Can Survive A Price War

Years ago, I ran a business where we had developed a groundbreaking product, called the MAX232. The product was so successful, that fourteen competitors eventually built what they believed were exact replicas of our MAX232.

Many of our competitors, including Texas Instruments and Analog Devices, were much bigger companies than we were. They had the ability to manufacture products at lower costs than we could.

Their strategies were obvious. TI, Analog Devices, and the others would offer their version of the MAX232 at a lower price than we would.

Despite the relentless price pressure, we maintained our market share. We also kept our gross margins above 70%.

As I look back, I realize that TI and ADI might have been able to crush us, but they didn't. The answer to why we beat our larger competitors explains both how you can defend yourself against a price oriented competitor, and how you can win with a price oriented strategy: You need to understand that it's almost always not about just having a lower price.

TI, ADI and the others would announce their replicas of our MAX232 at around a 15% discount to our products. Each time our competitors lowered their prices, we would also lower our prices in response.

This is where we did the right thing, and this is where TI and ADI blew it. Our larger competitors assumed we would just give up, as they kept lowering the price.

Instead, we kept innovating while they never did.

We kept coming up with new innovations and products that offered more value to our customers. This made the MAX232 less relevant over time, because we moved customers to newer and better products. TI and ADI were left in the dust.

It also shows the fatal flaw of just relying on TI's and ADI's lower price strategy.

You need to lower prices AND innovate, if you're going to win in a price sensitive market.

To this day I'll never understand why TI and ADI didn't try and leapfrog our position in the market. Instead, they seemed happy to just follow us. With their superior manufacturing capability, they might have won, if they had innovated.

The lesson I took away from a small, startup perspective, is that David can beat Goliath. You don't fight their strength (in this case, lower costs), but you take advantage of the inherent slowness that big companies operate with.

You can't be afraid to obsolete your own products.

Speed kills.

We moved at a rapid clip, introducing innovative products, which made our earlier products obsolete. By the time that TI and ADI eventually tried to replicate our latest product, we were on to the next thing.

They never did catch up. We dominated the market, building a $200 million/year business with gross margins greater than 70%.

ROUND 11: RAISING YOUR NEXT ROUND OF FUNDING IS NOT A GIVEN

Can You Avoid No Man's Land?
Your Startup Depends On It.

Have you ever found yourself in No Man's Land? You know. It's kind of like you're driving along on the highway, and a sign comes along: "Next gas, 50 miles."

Your tank is close to empty. You're wondering, "Can I make it another 50 miles?"

The temperature is close to 100 degrees outside. You turn off the air conditioner, because you know that it is burning fuel. You then open up the windows.

You start sweating because, it's 100 degrees outside. You need to get to the next gas station.

Welcome to the world of running an early stage startup.

Instead of gas, you're wondering if you have enough money to get to your next round of funding.

Sometimes, through no fault of your own, you find yourself in No Man's Land. You're asking yourself the question, "Should I raise money now, before I need the funding? or "Should I wait to raise my funding and potentially get a higher valuation?"

It's not so black and white is it?

There are other possibilities. Maybe you truly are in No Man's Land:

It's too early for you to raise money, because you haven't hit enough milestones.

You will not have enough money to prove out your company, if you wait to raise money.

What do you do, if you truly are in No Man's Land?

I would first like to tell a story about my time in No Man's Land.

I used to meet every Friday afternoon with Tina, who was our very able Controller.

Tina used to come into my office with a pile of checks for me to sign. The routine was that she would hand me the check, tell me what the payment was for, I would ask any questions and then I would sign or not sign the check.

We would then review where we were financially. We would talk about our revenue plan, spending plan and how much money we had left.

On this particular Friday, it was clear to Tina and me that we were going to run out of money, before we hit our next major milestone.

Tina, as she usually was, was way ahead of me. She

said, "We need to either cut spending or get a loan."

I looked at the numbers, and started to sweat. We were in No Man's Land.

Make no mistake about it, "No Man's Land" sucks.

The good news was we weren't going to run out of money for over 12 months. This gave us lots of time to maneuver.

There's an old adage regarding raising money or getting a loan. That adage is "raise money, when you don't need it."

Rule Number One: Always be looking way ahead.

You have to give yourself at least six months to one year (I recommend at least one year) to be able to raise your funding. Therefore, go back into that equation to figure out when your next funding round is likely to close.

What's your financial situation going to be like in six months to one year? Are you going to have enough money?

Back to my story...

Fortunately, we were way ahead of the game, because Tina was on top of things. She had worked at many other startups, so she knew the time to act was now.

Tina and I started going through our options.

Option A. Raise venture funding now.

I could see if there was a group of investors that we could give an "early look" at the company.

The company was doing well. We had momentum, and we had accomplished a lot. We just hadn't hit the major milestone that we thought we needed to hit, to easily raise more money.

I have sometimes tried to raise money too early. It has come back to bite me.

Remember that you only get one chance to make a first impression. If you do go out and raise money too early, it can put you in a bind.

This is a good time to pre-shop your deal. In other words, testing the market with a small group of investors is a good way to go, because you haven't gone to all your potential investors too soon.

We did have another option...

Option B. Get a loan.

We could go to the venture lenders, such as Silicon Valley Bank, and see if we could get a loan.

The good thing about getting a loan is that it will extend your runway by whatever the amount of money the loan is. The bad news about a loan, is that the interest and principle payments will increase your break-even revenue point.

We had a third option...

Option C. Cut spending.

To significantly cut spending (as with most start-ups), would mean cutting headcount. I really didn't want to cut the team, because it was outstanding. We were also pretty lean already.

There was another option:

Option D. Do an inside funding round.

VCs typically like an external investor to lead the next round of funding. There are a couple of reasons why VCs like to do this:

1. It reduces the risk for the existing investors. You have another set of deep pockets around the table. That's always good, just in case there is a crisis.

2. The new investor "prices the round." In other words, the new investor determines the new valuation of the company.

An inside round, where the existing investor puts more money into the company without adding any new investors, was still worth considering because we were doing well, and our investors were positive on the company.

There was, of course, one other option:

Option E. Wait to raise money.

In other words, we could hope that we have enough money to get to our next milestone, and then raise funding.

I am risk averse. Waiting reduces your options to just one thing. Yes, we would likely own more of the company, if we hit our milestones and waited to raise money.

However, what would happen if we ran out of money before we hit our milestones? What would happen, if the investing climate changed?

I've never liked "bet the company" strategies. Waiting to raise more money, sure felt like a bet the company strategy to me.

We decided to go with the two-pronged strategy of getting a loan and testing the waters with a small group of investors.

We were successful in getting the loan. Even better yet, we were able to get the first year of the loan as interest only.

No principle would be due for one year, so our payments would be low. Tina did a great job.

Remember that startup success is binary. You're either going to win really big, or you're not going to win really big.

Trying to time the market to milk every last percent of ownership, can actually keep you from achieving startup success. The last percent of ownership you're holding out for, really doesn't matter.

Think about it. Let's say you're one of the fortunate few that has a $1 billion exit. Is it really going to matter if you own 10% or 8% of the company?

You always want disproportionate positive upsides versus the downside. That's why pushing for the extra 2% ownership might be keeping you from the 8% you know you can achieve.

It is important to be pragmatic, when you are thinking about your financial future. Get all the money you can, when you can get it. That's the best way to avoid No Man's Land.

Why Trying to Limit Your Investors Ownership Doesn't Matter

One of the greatest lines in movie history was said in the classic, *All the President's Men*. The line is, "Follow the money."

The idea was that if you traced the trail of money, you would find out who was behind the Watergate break-in.

Well, "follow the money" also holds true, if you are starting a company. Here's how:

Whoever invests in your company, regardless of how much they own, now controls the company.

Guy Kawasaki is right. The second you take on outside funding, your investors control your company. Your percentage ownership or whatever crazy voting rights you dream up will not save you from being fired, if you do a bad job.

Your investors make the rules, as long as you need more money. Period.

If you don't believe me, ask Travis Kalanick. Travis had voting control of Uber. He couldn't be voted out as CEO.

Yet here Kalanick is now, the ex-CEO of Uber.

Uber needed more money to keep the company growing, but the investors grew tired of Kalanick. It was inevitable that Kalanick would lose this show-down, because Uber needed money to keep the company alive.

The price of the new money was that Kalanick no longer be the CEO of Uber.

The only way to stay CEO, is to do a great job as CEO.

I'm not saying you shouldn't try and keep as much of the company as you can. However, you should focus on what matters, which is how you and your team execute.

If you do a great job, then you've got nothing to worry about. Your investors will be thrilled that you are the one company in their portfolio that they don't have to worry about.

That's what you should aim for. Worrying about owning 51% of the company will just get you in trouble.

How Can I Make Sure My Startup Doesn't Go Out of Business?

You'll hear this phrase over and over again, if you start spending time with venture capitalists. What's the phrase?

"Startups are very fragile."

I used to discount that idea when I was younger, cockier and stupider. I knew what I was doing, or so I thought.

Now I realize just how sage those words are.

There are so many things that can kill your startup, when you are starting out. The challenge is you are single threaded in so many different areas, that a failure in any one of them can knock you out.

What are these areas? Let me give you three to think about:

A. Customer concentration.

Let's say you have one customer who accounts for 95% of your revenue when you are starting out. That's actually quite possible.

You staff up to take advantage of the revenue spike. Then guess what happens? Your large customer disappears, and you don't add any additional large customers.

You've now got double trouble, because you're burning money at a higher rate, and your revenue has dropped.

The answer is to run your company, as if the 95% revenue customer doesn't exist. If you can't do that because your business model depends upon large customers, then get as much of the money as you can from your large customers up front.

If customer concentration isn't the problem, then maybe this is:

B. Your VP Engineering or CTO walks out the door.

I had this happen, and it almost killed us.

Our VP Engineering quit, right before we were going to get funding. As a result, our funding was gone in an instant. The second challenge was that we had to replace the VP Engineering.

You are by definition single threaded, when you are starting out. Losing a key founder when you are just starting out, and you have a small team, can be a killer.

What do you do when you when lose your co-founder? What do you say when you lose your co-

founder?

You have to move fast when your co-founder quits. There's no time for regret. You have to move and find the replacement.

At the same time, don't settle. You should be looking to upgrade your team each and every time there is a departure.

At the same time, you need to be transparent with your team, investors and potential investors about your co-founder leaving the company. This gives you the ability to control the story.

If your team isn't the problem, maybe this is:

C. Your vendor screws you at absolutely the wrong time.

Of all the things that surprised me starting our company, it had to be the number of times a key vendor screwed us. None of the screwups were malicious, but each time a vendor screwed up, it cost us precious time.

What's the answer? Try to have multiple vendors, as much as possible.

For example, in manufacturing our products, we had multiple test and assembly facilities. This strategy saved us many times.

I wish we could have done the same thing with our fabs, but that just isn't possible in today's world.

As you can see, there are many things that can kill you, when you're an early stage startup. The good news is that you can recover from many of these problems, if you jump on them.

Stop Wasting Your Time Looking For Value Added Investors

I remember having a conversation with my Dad, when I became an Entrepreneur in Residence (EIR) at a San Francisco based venture capital firm. The VC firm had hired me to build a company, and we were just about ready to start raising money.

I told my Dad, "We only want to raise money from Tier 1 VCs because they will bring so much more to the table than Tier 2 and Tier 3 VCs."

My Dad laughed and said to me, "Brett, everyone's money is green."

My Dad was so right. Investors are just that, investors. You want their money and their support. Anything else positive is a bonus.

I remember feeling very nervous before our first board of director's meeting, after we closed our funding. Dave, my advisor and coach, had suggested that I meet with each investor and board member 1:1 before each board meeting.

I still worried and wondered what we would discuss in these meetings. Would there be deep strategic discussions about the direction of the business?

Would the board meeting last six or eight hours?

My investors were experienced investors from arguably Tier 1 firms. I think they got, and I got, much more out of our 1:1 meetings, than the board meetings. The board meetings had the feel of a necessary evil, something you had to do, but the meetings were of little value.

You want to get in, get out, and get done.

I remember asking Gill, one of my investors, in one of our 1:1 meetings, if we should have a strategic discussion in the board meeting about the direction we were taking. Gill said, "Well, we can do that if you like. But you need to have a clear idea of what you want to do."

In other words, he was saying, "Don't expect us to solve your problems, because you might not like what we come up with."

As time went on, I realized the true value of our board meetings was giving our board a chance to interact with the executive team. That was not at all what I would have expected, but that's what it was.

I made a huge effort to never, ever surprise the board. I think the transparency helped us build trust. Beyond that, I felt that our board meetings were something we had to do. Get in, get out, and get done as fast as possible was my goal.

You should expect your investors to provide you with strategic advice.

I was fortunate to have two experienced investors, but their styles couldn't have been more different. It was, as Regis McKenna told me (he was an advisor to Gill's fund and he had worked with our other investor, "Raul"), "The yin and the yang."

Gill liked to gently guide me. Raul liked to dictate. However, for the most part, they just let me run the company as I saw fit. They were almost like guardrails.

That is how it should be. You are the CEO. It's your company to run.

It's your company, so you are under no obligation to follow the advice.

For example, I felt we needed to get a loan to extend our runway, before we raised our next round of funding. I had Tina, our controller, work with Silicon Valley Bank to arrange the financing.

I obviously needed our investors approval, so I spoke with Gill and Raul in our 1:1s. Raul agreed with my decision instantly, but I was surprised that Gill was against the idea.

"We've seen eye to eye about everything until now," I said.

"I know," Gill responded. "I think you're better off

just raising the next round. However, I'll support you, if this is what you want to do."

The most powerful thing your investors can bring to the table is their support and alignment with you.

That's what I loved about Gill. He understood that it was your company to run as CEO, not his. Every step of our journey together, he supported us.

Alignment. That's what you really, really want from your investors. When you have alignment, you can move mountains and build a really great company.

When you don't have alignment, it's like you're fighting a world champion boxer with one hand tied behind your back. Just remember that investors are not your friends, they are investors.

As my Dad said to me, "Everyone's money is green." You just want to make sure the money keeps flowing.

ROUND 12: SCALING YOUR BUSINESS LOOKS EASY. IT'S NOT.

What Are The Most Important
Things To Keep In Mind,
When Scaling Your Startup?

"We're in the first stage of a three-stage fab expansion," "Bob," the CEO, proudly told me.

It was December 2000, and I was being recruited to run the Communication's Division of Bob's company. The economic bubble was bursting already, yet here was this CEO boldly proclaiming his company was expanding.

"Do you really think this is the right time?" I asked. "The 'comms' bubble appears to be bursting."

"Hogwash!" (Yes, Bob actually said Hogwash). "The market is going to come back strong in 2001. I know it will!"

Six months later, the company put the fab expansion on hold.

Nine months later, the company went through a massive layoff.

Determining when to scale and when to pull back, is one of the most difficult things you need to do as a

CEO. If you scale too quickly, you can end up hurting a lot of people. If you scale too slowly, you can miss your opportunity.

As much as I want to blame Bob for what was clearly a faulty decision, I can't do it.

The answer of when to scale or not to scale is never, ever clear.

It's even more difficult, if you're running a startup. Scaling too fast can cost you your company, if you're wrong.

The Dangers of Premature Scaling of Your Company.

What is the one decision you want to avoid?

At all costs, you want to avoid what I call a "bet the company" decision. A bet the company decision is literally a decision where your company will go away, if you're wrong.

But startups are meant to be all or nothing propositions. Right?

Not exactly.

The likelihood that your original idea will work exactly as you thought it would is really low. There's always some tweaking or pivoting of your original idea that will happen.

The key is leaving yourself enough runway (cash)

to execute the pivots.

It usually takes at least two to three times longer for a startup to scale than the CEO/founder (that's you, btw) thinks it will. We entrepreneurs are an optimistic bunch, but your optimism can kill you if you are not careful.

I went through this when I was building my company. I had built businesses like the one I was building before. However, I was still surprised at how long it took to get to scale.

The problem wasn't that we had the wrong products. The problem wasn't that customers didn't love us. It just takes time.

What do you do? Look for the signs.

You need to look at the micro signs (that's what your company is doing) and the macro signs (the external environment).

First, let's talk about the two important micro-signs to look for when you are looking if this is the right time to scale:

A. Customer feedback.

In the early days of your company, relentlessly pursuing customer feedback should be at the top of your goals. You need to know why customers are buying your products. You also need to know if you are really easing their pain points.

Just as important, you need to understand why customers aren't buying, what's wrong with your product or service and what needs to be improved.

In other words, you're looking for that elusive product market fit. Product market fit is kind of like what Supreme Court justice Potter Stewart said about pornography. You'll know it, when you've got it.

The goal at the early stage isn't for every customer to love everything about your product. That will never happen. The goal is for enough of the customers to be giving you enough positive feedback that you know you are onto something. One of the critical ways that you know you have achieved product market fit is:

B. You have a repeatable and predictable sales process.

You're looking for your customers to buy in a logical and repeatable fashion. Logical and repeatable doesn't mean that two customers in a row have bought from you.

Logical and repeatable does mean that a consistent number of customers are buying from you over a significant period of time. More importantly, your customers are buying through a repeatable and potentially scalable methodology you are using.

This likely means that your first group of customers

doesn't fall in this category. More often than not, your first group of customers are acquired through your hustle.

Maybe you're cold calling customers. Maybe you're going to meet ups. These are great ways to get an initial customer base.

However, cold calling and going to meet ups are not scalable. You don't yet have a repeatable, scalable process.

Don't jump the gun on when you're seeing a logical and repeatable pattern. This is probably one of the biggest mistakes you can make.

I'd much rather gradually scale and lose some sales in the process, then go all in too early and potentially lose my company. There's nothing wrong with leaving a little business on the table. You will not give up your competitive advantage.

Be wary of investors telling you, "Don't worry, we'll support you."

Investors love saying, "Don't worry, we'll support you." They truly mean it...until something changes, and they don't support you or they can't support you anymore.

It's easy to get swayed. Believe me, I know. However, you need look no further than the current funding environment for why it's so important to not ramp up too quickly.

Remember that ramping up burns cash. Cash is the lifeblood of your company.

Now, let's talk macro signs.

Markets are usually moving in relatively predictable ways. What do you do when they aren't? And more importantly, how do you know you're in a market environment like the bubble of 1999, or the Great Recession of 2008?

First, you look for early warning signs.

I'm not going to lie to you. Identifying the early warning signs can be really difficult.

The key is to be aware of what's going on around you. For example, the startup fund raising environment has recently become more difficult. This means that it's likely going to take you longer to raise money (if you can raise money at all), so your cash is going to have to last longer.

 How did I know that the fundraising environment has recently become more difficult? This one wasn't hard. It's been all over the press and many people in the startup ecosystem are talking about it.

Many times, it's more difficult. I remember raising money in 2008. At that time, the signs there was a problem were very gradual.

However, the signs were there. Now you have tools, like Google Trends, to help you. For example, insert recession into Google Trends and look at what pops up:

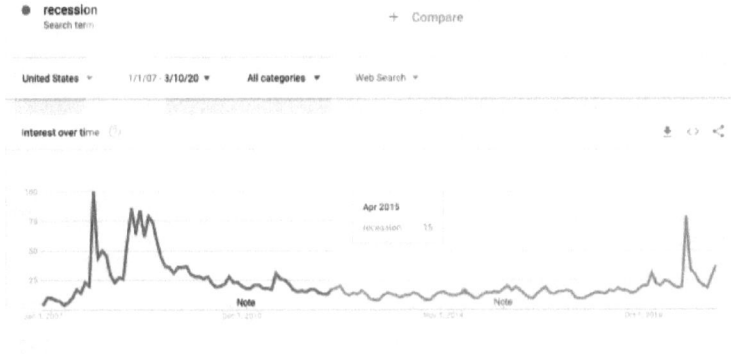

Wow! There it is! Clear as a bell, in January 2008, there was a lot of concern about a recession.

Second, you always conserve your cash.

Cash is about the only thing you have complete control over as a CEO. The general rule is pretty simple.

You should always conserve your cash.

You may miss the warning signs of an oncoming crisis. The market might suddenly turn. or you might have been dependent upon one customer for 80% of your revenue and that customer cancels their business with you.

All of these problems and more can happen.

That's why you conserve your cash. When you are scaling, you really need to watch your cash.

You should ask yourself, how much cash is it going to cost you to scale? Will you have any cash left, if the scaling doesn't work as planned?

The key with scaling is to expect that the scaling will not go as planned. Therefore, you need to make sure you have cash to weather whatever follows.

What should be the limiting factor on your growth?

Let's say the scaling went reasonably well. Your business is growing, and you're in a good cash position.

Should you continue scaling, and what should be the limiting factors on your growth?

I'll give you a one-word answer: People.

Your ability to continue recruiting top-notch people should be the limiting factor on your growth. Hiring mediocre people or people that don't fit your culture might not initially hurt your company. However, in the long run, hiring mediocre people will significantly hurt your company.

I've seen what dropping your hiring standards can do.

Years ago, I was working for a very successful company, Maxim Integrated Products. The team was 80% A level players and 20% B and C level players.

Maxim was able to maintain that incredibly high talent ratio to about $500 million/year in revenue. The founding CEO, the late Jack Gifford, then started hiring outsiders to fill General Manager roles.

Gifford had previously promoted from within to fill General Manager roles. The newly hired outsider GM's had two problems:

1. They were not A level players.
2. They didn't fit the company's unique culture.

Each new general manager, just like the existing general managers, was goaled on his ability to hire engineers. The new general managers met their hiring goals.

Just to be clear, Gifford made very few mistakes as CEO. However, this was one of them. Gifford assumed that the talent level of the new hires would be the same as in the past. It wasn't. Many of these new hires were people we would have passed on previously.

It took a few years, but all of these general managers failed. The company still has not recovered to this day.

That's why you need to make hiring the limiting factor on your growth.

Scaling, as you can see, is tough.

The first CEO we talked about, Bob, blew it, by not monitoring the macro economic climate. The second CEO, Jack Gifford, blew it, by hiring the wrong people.

You can avoid scaling mistakes, by watching the signs. Watch the micro signs (your company's growth metrics) and macro signs (the economy) for clues.

You should also always leave yourself a cash buffer, in case things don't go according to plan. Finally, never, ever lower your hiring standards, because you will eventually pay the price.

What Are the Keys To Successful Minimum Viable Products?

There's a lot of misinformation out there about Minimum Viable Products (MVPs). This includes a belief that it's the right way to go if you develop an MVP, because people are naturally going to buy your product. I want to debunk this idea right now.

Just because you develop an MVP, does not necessarily mean your product is going to sell. I think this is a really important thing for you to think about.

There has to be value in the MVP. In fact, there has to be significant value in the MVP.

This is how I want you to think about MVPs. Your product has to have, if you're starting out or this is your first, second or third product, something significantly better about the product or you can't release it.

In other words, the MVP you release has to be 10X to 100X better than what is available today.

You will fail if you introduce an MVP, and it has no redeeming feature. You can save money. The product can also be simple to develop.

However, I don't care whether it is a hardware product or a software product.

Guess what's going to happen, if there's nothing better about the MVP? Your MVP is not going to sell.

You will have wasted whatever money you spent on your MVP.

This is one of the points I want to drive home today. Just developing an MVP because an MVP is on a checklist of what you're supposed to do, does not guarantee you success.

Make sure that the simplest product you're going to develop and produce has significant value. Otherwise, you need to rethink your development plan.

What's the difference between a prototype and an MVP?

A prototype is going to be something simple that may or may not be ready for your customers to use. An MVP, by contrast, is a product that you've tested and done the work to sell the product to the public.

Prototypes are for internal use.

Sometimes you may provide prototypes to your customers to show them what you're up to. Always make sure to tell your customers that it is just a prototype.

Make sure the customer knows the product is not

yet for sale, has not been extensively tested, and that you are interested in getting the customer's honest feedback. I've done this with Alpha and Beta products, and I've gotten very good feedback.

I would then tell customers when the product is going to be released to production. You can get very useful feedback, by engaging early with your customers.

You want to be thinking about developing a product that is useful to your customers. Remember that the product has to be significantly better or your customers are going to roll their eyes and move on.

You will have wasted whatever amount of time and money you have spent, on something that isn't going to sell.

There has to be redeeming value in whatever you develop, and your MVP has to be significantly better, if it's going to sell.

What is the minimum amount you have to have developed, before you can start talking about your startup?

The question you have is whether you need a pitch deck, before you start talking to customers? Do you need an alpha version or beta version of your product before you start talking to customers?

One of the big mistakes I see entrepreneurs make, is

they wait too long before they start talking to potential customers. You want to look at things, like there is a giant feedback loop out there.

The quicker you get feedback and adjust, the quicker you can make whatever changes you need to make. I don't care what kind of product you're doing, your goal is how can you get paying customers as quickly as possible?

I was just having a conversation about the benefits of getting out there quickly, with someone I am working with. He's been working for a while on his MVP.

The point I was making with him, is that he needs to start getting in front of customers and get someone to start paying for what he is doing. The biggest validation you can get is having someone start paying you for your products.

It doesn't matter if your first customer pays a highly discounted rate for your product (say $10 for a product that is worth $200). Getting someone to pay for your product, is a huge validation that you are on the right track.

Think about the steps that you need to take in your business to get those answers (ideally a paying customer) as quickly as possible. Your goals are making customers aware of what you are doing and getting them to start buying.

You can start making adjustments, once you get

customer feedback. That's when you begin to make use of the minimum viable information.

This minimum viable information (both positive and negative) gives you the vital initial reaction you need to keep moving forward. You can now learn and adapt more quickly.

The whole concept behind minimum viable products really should be how do you get useful answers from the market as inexpensively and quickly as possible.

There has to be something significantly different about what you're doing with that minimum set of product features, or you're not going to get any useful feedback. If you can't get customers excited by what you're doing, then:

- The differentiation of your product isn't significant enough., or...

- Your product isn't unique in an area that your customer base cares about, or...

- You may be focused on the wrong market or customer base.

You will get this necessary market feedback quickly, if you use the strategy I outlined above. You can then make the adjustments you need to make as fast as possible.

What is the maximum amount of time you should

spend building your MVP?

This is a broad question, so let me try and make it as specific as possible. In one sense, the answer is how quickly can you develop a product that is unique and differentiated enough, so you can get useful answers.

You should follow the concept of stripping the product down, so you identify the key feature or features your customers need. Customers don't make decisions on five or six things that you are doing. Customers make decisions on one or two key features. That's what sells products.

It doesn't matter whether your product is a physical or software product, or a service, it's those one or two unique things that you do significantly better than everyone else that will sell your product. That's what customers can keep in their minds.

If you start trying to sell your product on four or five or six features, that's far too many features. You want to strip down what you're doing, so those one or two key features can stand out.

Your product can then be useful to customers in its minimal form. This will allow you to get to that point with the least amount of effort.

It's fantastic if you can get to this point, because now you know the minimum amount of time you need to develop your first product(s). It is important to remember that the one or two features you choose to focus on need to be significantly different.

You will likely fail, if your product isn't significantly different. It will not matter how well- meaning you are, nor how strong your customer relationships are. You need to reset your thought process, if you cannot determine the one or two features that make your product unique.

How do you test your minimum viable product?

In other words, "Do I really need to test as rigorously as the final product that I develop?" Let me give you a simple analogy for anything you release to market.

You only get one chance to make a first impression.

This is your baby. This is your company. You're going out to the real world and saying, "Look at me. I've got this really cool product. It's unique. It's different. You know what? It works!"

Therefore, you need to do as much testing as you would do on your final product for your minimum viable product. Your product needs to be tested rigorously and thoroughly, so you know all the areas that are problematic before the product goes out.

Hopefully, whatever those areas are, if it makes the product unusable, then you don't want to be out there selling the product. This is the difference between a prototype and production.

Remember that your minimum viable product is a production product.

Prototypes can have all sorts of issues. You can go to your customers and say, "I have a prototype right here, and you can evaluate it for free. It has these known problems."

However, if you are selling a production product, the product problems you have cannot get in the way of the use of the product. You need to make sure that the product is tested thoroughly, so none of these problems come out in production.

About the worst thing that can happen to you, is you're caught unaware of a product problem. This can be worse than not going out with the product at all.

You want to be really careful because if you burn your customers, they start using something that doesn't work and you don't know it doesn't work, then you must start backtracking. A product problem that you don't know about, can be really tough on your company.

That is why you thoroughly test your product. It allows you to understand all the issues and all the corner cases that may happen. When you're prepared, you can make an informed decision about releasing the product.

You need to be very "open kimono" with your customers about any potential problems. That means you need to be very open and honest that in certain applications, your product is going to work in a suboptimal way.

You are now being honest, and you're getting ahead of the issue. Customers will now respect you for your transparency. However, if the customer finds the problem before you do, you can get in trouble.

It gets very difficult when you are trying to build a company and a brand, when you are dealing with product problems. Every company that ever existed (including both hardware and software companies) will have issues with products.

Every company I've been involved with, has had product issues. Having said that, we tell our customers as soon as we find the issues.

You get ahead of the problems. That's how you continue building strong relationships with your customers.

How narrow or limited should your MVP be?

The test for how narrow or limited your MVP should be is very simple. The question is, "Is what I'm doing significantly different in a meaningful way to my customers?"

This is really a 1/0, Yes/No question.

Go forward, if your MVP is significantly different.

You need to stop your development, if your MVP isn't significantly different.

I don't how cheap it is to develop your MVP, but you need to stop if you don't have significant advantage. Your MVP isn't going to sell, and you're not going to gain much, if any, useful feedback on your next generation product.

Worse, all of your effort, money and time will go for naught. That's what you're trying to avoid.

When you think about minimum viable products, you need to be thinking that you have to have something different. That difference may be a subset of what you want to build out later.

That difference may also be a subset of your long-term plan. However, your MVP needs to be unique or it's just not going to sell.

This means you're wasting your time, if your MVP is not unique.

I've seen this throughout my career. I've made these mistakes, and I don't want you to make the same ones.

Any product that sold, especially in the early days of a company I was involved in, was really different. I like to use this minimum of 10X.

The product needs to be better by a factor of at least 10X on something. That's when you start getting attention.

It's very easy to delude yourself into believing that your product will sell, if you're 10-20% better than the competition. You say to yourself, "We're a little better than the competition. We're going to be aggressive. We're going to discount the price."

This strategy rarely works.

What works is when you are so much better than the competition that customers are willing to take a chance on using your product. This tells you the limitations of what you can and cannot do.

You can start adding other features to your product later. You must have enough (think 10X better) to make it worthwhile for your customers to work with you.

Put yourself in the customer's shoes. We've all been customers before. We are taking risks, when we buy a product from a new brand.

The question your customers are asking is, "Why am I taking risks from what I'm using before to this new brand?"

The answer is always the same. "It's so much better than what's out there, that it is worth me taking the risk."

This is how you need to think about your customers. You need to put yourself in the shoes of your customers, in terms of why customers are going to work with you.

You need to brutally honest with yourself about what those reasons are. Because if the answer isn't unequivocally, "Yes, I'm willing to take this risk. I'm willing to this chance on this unknown brand," they are not going to take the risk on using your product.

What do you do after the minimum viable product? Well, it's obviously the next generation of products.

Let's rephrase the question a little bit. What do you want to do and what are your goals with your MVP?

A. You want to start getting people to buy from you.

This is the point where you are in a go or no-go phase, in terms of what you are doing. You want people to start paying you something.

It doesn't have to be full price, but you want proof that customers will buy from you. And...

B. You want to start gaining feedback.

You can gain considerable feedback about customers like about your product, what they dislike about your product, what they want to see you do next, pricing and the competition. You can gain this information from the work you've done.

Now you can learn:

- What do you do next

- Where do you go next

- What customers are you resonating with

- What customers aren't you resonating with

- What is working

- What isn't working

That is the beauty of this type of iterative approach, if you use it right. You already have a roadmap of what products come next with what features.

Your MVP and the feedback you get from your MVP, help you make the needed adjustments to your plan. You can now spend your hard-earned money with more certainty.
You can now add features, based on the feedback you've received, and make pivots. Pivoting doesn't necessarily mean making radical changes to your plan.

Pivoting can involve small changes to your plan and your products. However, these small changes can be the difference between success and failure.

You want to be gathering information. You want to be in constant communication with your customers. Get feedback from your customers, and learn more about then.

You want to under-promise and over-deliver!

Oh, what a beautiful way to run your business. Under-promising and over-delivering means that your customers will always be pleasantly surprised.

What is the key to making the most of your minimum viable product?

Your MVP needs to significantly different than what is available in today's marketplace. You want to be 10X different as a minimum number.

Focus on those one or two key features that make your MVP unique. That's what's going to make your company stand out from everything else out there.

You want to really tough on yourself. Be brutally honest about whether your product is truly 10X better.

Don't go forward, if your product doesn't stand out. Go forward and get feedback as fast as you can, if your product does stand out.

It's that differentiation in a meaningful way that will allow your customers to take a chance on your new company. This is the key to making your minimum viable products work.

Even before you release your MVP, start testing your ideas with customers. Don't be afraid to start testing your ideas early. and to get pre-orders from your customers.

The quicker you get confirmation that you're on to something, means the quicker you can move forward. You can also make the needed adjustments to your plan faster, if the feedback is negative.

You have a much better chance of success, if you take these steps.

Why You Shouldn't Follow the Lean Startup Methodology?

I was at work, when I heard that Steve Jobs died. Vivi, our layout manager, told me her husband (who worked at Apple) called to let her know.

I felt sad. I'd only briefly met Steve once.

Blossom, Avery and I were getting smoothies at Whole Foods in Palo Alto. Avery was about two years old, and she was running around amusing herself.

I looked up from watching Avery, and I saw Steve Jobs staring right at us. He smiled at Blossom and me and mouthed, "She's cute."

Jobs got his smoothie and walked away.

Today, Blossom sent me a video that included Jobs' famous Stanford University commencement speech. The bit that was included was Jobs' reference to thinking different.

This brings me to two important topics: Lean Startups and Minimum Viable Products.

The concept of the lean startup has always been part of the startup vocabulary. Long before it was made popular and the book was written, many entrepreneurs were following the basic concepts of the lean startup.

Let me quote from Wikipedia:

"The central hypothesis of the lean startup methodology is that if startup companies invest their time into iteratively building products or services to meet the needs of early customers, they can reduce the market risks and sidestep the need for large amounts of initial project funding and expensive product launches and failures."

The concept is simple and logical to follow:

 You just:

Develop the simplest version of your product that you can think of.

This is your Minimum Viable Product (MVP). Then...

Listen to what the market is telling you and gather feedback.

Then...

Make whatever adjustments you need to make to your MVP for the next version of the product based on market feedback. You could even pivot away from your original idea to a new idea.

Then...

Go through steps A through C for the rest of the life of the company again and again.

You're saying, "What's the problem? The lean startup model sounds like a great way to start a company."

You're right. The framework of the lean startup is a good framework, but...

Too many entrepreneurs are following the Lean Startup methodology and failing. Why is that?

I remember after Steve Jobs died, there were stories of all these wannabe Steve Jobs that kept popping up. I remember one particular story of this wannabe Jobs, who started wearing black mock turtlenecks (like the ones Jobs wore) after Jobs died.

What was this fellow thinking? Did this CEO truly think the magic was in the turtleneck?

Be Different.

The magic in following the lean startup formula (or any other formula for that matter) isn't in blindly following the formula. It's the creativity that you put on top of the formula that allows you to win.

I've seen far too many companies blindly follow the lean startup methodology. The companies release their MVPs, only to get no traction.

The failures are all similar. There was nothing or

not enough different about their product compared to the competition.

Remember your MVP needs to be off the charts better than what's available!

Think about it.

You need to stand out:

You need to be at least 10X better than your competitors. And...

That means your MVP has to be at least 10X better than your competitors.

Clayton Christenson's masterpiece, The Innovator's Dilemma dramatizes how MVPs can work:

- Usually the first-generation product has a flaw(s) versus the competition.

- However, that flaw is not that important to an emerging market segment.

- Therefore, your product can gain traction in the emerging segment.

- While making improvements in the imperfections.

- Eventually you dominate the whole market!

Think Different.

For example, consider the original iPhone.

Let's go back to Jobs.

The iPhone was seriously flawed compared to the incumbent Blackberry. The keyboard and security were barely good enough.

However, the user experience was much better. Jobs also brilliantly focused on the consumer market that Blackberry didn't care about.

Combine a brilliant plan with a complacent competitor (Blackberry), and the new entrant (Apple) ends up dominating the mobile phone market.

Apple clearly had lots of money to spend on the development of the iPhone. However, that's not the point.

The point is that your company and its products or services need to be different in a meaningful way.

Differentiation can come in many different ways, shapes and forms. For example, you can:

Have a differentiated product like the iPhone versus the Blackberry, or...

You can have a differentiated market focus, like the iPhone focusing on the consumer market versus the Blackberry focusing on the business market. Or...

You can have a differentiated manufacturing model, where your product costs significantly less to produce or deliver to your customers. You can then pass on the savings to your customers.

However, you have to be different in a way that is meaningful to your customers.

How can you use the lean startup formula and win?

Every situation is different. I don't like having a one size fits all approach to things. However, there are general rules you should always follow as a cash-strapped startup:

- Conserve your cash.
- Don't spend on lavish parties.
- Buy used furniture.
- As CEO, sign every check.

Focus on being appropriately frugal.

A philosophy of being appropriately frugal means you:

A. Save money where you can.

You don't need fancy office furniture, a chef, or a bunch of schwag. Save money where possible. Not only will you extend your runway, you set an example for your team of not wasting.

B. You need to spend on what's important.

The most important thing to spend money on (usually), is your team. Don't scrimp on hiring a great team that fits your culture.

C. Make sure your MVP is differentiated.

An MVP that isn't differentiated in a meaningful way is worthless. You've wasted time and money, if you develop an undifferentiated MVP.

Spend the money (in team and resources) that you need to develop a truly differentiated MVP. You will then get to market as inexpensively as possible with a truly unique product.

Conclusion:

I remember meeting with one of our investors. Gill was telling me that some of his portfolio company CEOs felt that the secret to startup success was:

- Wearing hoodies
- Having blowout parties

I could tell by the tone in his voice and the look in his eyes that he did not approve. Gill said to me:

"Mark Zuckerberg is successful because, well, he's Mark Zuckerberg, not because he wears hoodies.

"Steve Jobs was successful because he was Steve Jobs, not because he wore black turtlenecks."

People sometimes put style over substance. Without substance, style doesn't matter.

Developing a successful MVP is part art and part science. The science is the easy part, because you just need to know the market you are going after.

The art is the skill Steve Jobs had; the ability to interpret what the market was really saying. Did the market really want a phone with true internet browsing capability?

Probably not. The market feedback Apple most likely had was, "Give us an improved keyboard compared to the Blackberry."

How Do You Turnaround and Rebuild Your Company?

"Bring us up to your level," "Bob," the CEO, said to me in his office. Bob was pitching me on becoming general manager of one of the company's three business units.

I smiled, we shook hands and I left his office. The truth was that I wasn't sold on whether I wanted to work with Bob. I had another offer to become a partner at a San Francisco-based VC firm.

I was trying to decide between the two offers. On the one hand, becoming a VC could be a lot of fun and I would learn a lot. On the other hand, I wasn't sure I wanted to stop being operational at this point in my career.

Therefore, despite my lack of certainty about Bob and his company, I decided to stay operational and become GM of Bob's communication's division. I let Mike, the Managing Partner at the VC fund, know I would not join the VC fund, and we agreed to keep in touch.

You have to be excited by the prospect of executing a turnaround.

My good friend, Steve, was already working in the division I was taking over. Steve let me know that there was a lot of work to be done.

I wasn't surprised by what I was getting into. However, Bob kept telling me how great a situation I would be taking over.

Who did I believe? Steve, of course.

I had a pretty good idea of how I was going to attack the situation. There were five steps in the process, and I'll bet you'll likely also have many of the same steps in your turnaround process.

Turnaround Step One: You need to meet with the team you inherited.

I remember that first meeting with my seven direct reports. They were, to put it mildly, an eclectic group.

I was left with two impressions after that first meeting:

A. Their morale was really low.

No one in the group, with the exception of Steve who was traveling, thought they could do anything well. When I talked to the marketing people, they said, "We're marketing. Nothing's expected of us."

When I talked with the engineering people, they said, "We just produce mediocre products."

It was a downer being around these people. The other issue was that we were in this big building several miles away from the main campus.

It felt like a morgue. There was no energy in the

building, because it was sparsely populated, and we were spread out throughout the building. In between, there was nothing but empty cubicles.

My first action was an easy one: Move everyone into the same area, so we could start collaborating together and get some energy going.

Getting everyone together would allow me to see if my second realization was correct:

B. The team didn't seem that good.

I've worked with older teams before that could run circles around their younger counterparts. In this case, it seemed that we had an older team that was just trying to hang on until retirement.

After that first meeting, I met one on one with each member of the team. Unsurprisingly to me, the older team members each tried to play me, by talking a great game.

I knew the truth would win out over time, and it did. At first, their effort was really strong. However, as month one turned into month two, and month two into month three, it became clear that the team I inherited would likely have to be replaced.

Turnaround Step Two: Analyze the simple details of your business.

One of the mantras I've seen hold true with every business I've been involved in, is that, at its core, business is usually very simple. You rarely need to look for complex problems to solve.

Instead, you can start by looking for the simple problems that needed to be solved. It became instantly clear that, besides the personnel issues, no customers were aware of the business' new product introductions.

It only took me one day to figure out what the problem was. I asked the Marketing Manager, Michelle, where was all the collateral for the products we'd introduced in the past 12 months.

Michelle said, "There isn't any."

I did a triple take. "What do you mean, 'there isn't any.' How do they sell new products without any documentation?"

"I don't know," she said. "I just know there isn't any documentation."

I was dumbfounded. I wondered, "How can you run a business this way?"

"What about advertisements?" I asked. "What was the last product they advertised?"

"Let me look," Michelle said. She looked at her database. "It's been over two years, since they advertised a new product."

"Unbelievable," I said, shaking my head.

The good news was that this was an extremely fixable problem. At the same time, I was sad. It was like no one cared. No one did care, except for my friend Steve.

When Steve got back from his trip, I told him what I had found. Then I said, "You must be going crazy here."

Steve just nodded.

Turnaround Step Three: Know your numbers.

In parallel with fixing the system problems I found, I started digging into the financials. I wasn't looking for complicated problems. I was going to start with simple problems.

I didn't have to look far. Most of the business unit's products were sold through distributors, so I wanted to look at the distributors "Point of Sale," or POS, reports for clues. "Charles," the Distribution Director, refused to give them to me.

"That's interesting," I said to myself. I then called the VP of Sales and I asked him to provide me with the reports.

"You don't need that information," he said to me.

"This is getting more interesting," I said to myself. I literally had to explain to the VP of Sales why I needed the information, before he relented.

Looking at the reports, it became clear that Charles had been, what's called, "stuffing the channel." The company recognized revenue when product was shipped to the distributor, not when the distributor sold the product.

Without any checks and balances in the system (and this company had no checks on anything), an unscrupulous manager, like Charles, could pump up his numbers (and thus pump up his bonus) if he could get distributors to agree to accept more product.

Think of this kind of like a mini Ponzi scheme. You can operate the scheme by shipping more inventory to distributors than they need, as long as demand is high. However, once demand drops, look out below.

That's exactly what happened. I could see that end customer consumption was well below what we were shipping to distributors. Then, inevitably, the distributors started shipping back their excess inventory to us, because their contracts allowed them to.

Before revenue bottomed out, we had a quarter where we actually had negative bookings. I didn't even know that was possible.

What a mess. However, this was a fixable problem.

Turnaround Step Four: You're going to need to cut people and cut products.

It was clear to me that most of the team would have to go. The good news for me was that the company was struggling, and we were planning on doing a lay-off.

I took advantage of the layoff to let go of most of the staff. I moved Steve to a central role as my number two, and we were off and running.

My analysis into the products made it clear that they'd gotten into end markets, where they had no real competitive advantage. The results were predictable. None of the products were selling.

Turnaround Step Five: You'll need to rebuild.

I now knew everything I needed to do. I set up a meeting with Bob and the CFO to explain to him the recovery plan for the business. I thought Bob would be thrilled, but I was wrong.

I started explaining everything I saw and how to fix it to Bob.

"Now you've done it," Bob said, after I explained the lack of collateral.

"Now you've done it," Bob said, after I explained the personnel issues.

"Now you've done it," Bob said, after I explained the issues with distribution.

Then Bob got up, straightened his tie, and said to

me, "I never want to have another meeting like this again with you."

Then he left.

I realized why I was uneasy with Bob, when I met him months ago in his office. Bob was all about Bob's ego being massaged.

Bob was the emperor with no clothes. He literally couldn't handle being told anything was wrong with his company.

I never did have another meeting like that with Bob again. I spent the rest of my time at the company turning the division from the least profitable, and money losing division of the company into the most profitable division of the company. I did it without ever telling Bob what I was up to.

Then Bob fired me. One of the first people I contacted after I was fired was Mike, the Managing Director of San Francisco VC fund. Mike asked me to become an Entrepreneur in Residence (EIR). My mission was to start a new company in the space. The effort led to me starting my own company.

What Is the Biggest Management Mistake You've Ever Made?

I blew it. The voice in the back of my head was arguing with itself. On the one hand, it was saying, "Don't hire 'Tom.' There's something wrong with him."

On the other hand, the voice was saying, "Brett, you need help in this area. You should hire Tom. He's got a wealth of experience. The whole board has interviewed him and loves him. Two board members have worked with him previously. He'll help close funding. Just do it, Brett! Hire Tom."

The first voice said to the second voice, "Brett, he's all of those things, but he's just a little off. Are you really sure about this?"

The second voice in my head said, "Yes, I'm sure about this. I am going to make an offer to Tom."

Then I hired him.

Months later, as we were in the process of closing funding, Tom told me that he had consulted a few years ago for another venture-backed company. I didn't remember seeing it on Tom's CV.

The chairman of the venture-backed company was a personal friend, so I called Winston and asked about Tom. Here's what I heard:

- Tom was an employee, not a consultant.

- Tom was fired after six months on the job.

Tom clearly had lied to me. Just as importantly, Tom had withheld information on his CV.

Tom had to leave the company.

So, what did I do? I didn't immediately fire Tom. That was my big mistake.

You have to fire problem employees, especially senior executives, quickly.

We were in the middle of fundraising, and I convinced myself that firing a senior executive that we just hired would cause us trouble. Tom was failing at his job.

Tom wasn't doing what I asked him to do. In fact, Tom seemed downright incompetent. However, the board seemed to like Tom and our potential new investors kept asking about Tom, so I didn't fire him.

I was afraid of the consequences of firing Tom. I hoped that he would do an adequate job. I would then fire him after our funding closed.

Problem employees always create problems at the absolute worst time.

You can guess what happened next. Tom quit.

I called our existing investors to let them know that Tom was leaving. Our existing investors were so scared about Tom quitting, that they told me to not tell our new investors.

I didn't like this dynamic at all, because I would be lying to our new investors. That's not the way to build trust in a new relationship.

I called our new investors, and I let them know that Tom would be leaving the company. The responses went like this:

"Thanks for letting me know. Our diligence told us he might not work out. We appreciate your honesty."

Hah!

There are a few of lessons you can take from this experience:

A. Don't hesitate to fix bad personnel decisions.

Time will only make these bad decisions worse, not better.

B. Ignoring the voice in your head, especially regarding personnel decisions, can be catastrophic.

Having a senior person leave during fund raising can potentially cost you the funds, so we could have lost everything. Fortunately, it didn't.

C. Magnifying a mistake by hiding it, especially from your investors, can make things even worse.

Imagine what could have potentially happened, if I hadn't been honest with our new investors and they found out later? Never be afraid to tell the truth.

I should have listened to the voice in my head. There are three other things I should have done to prevent the mistake of hiring Tom from happening in the first place:

A. Reference checks.

I figured I didn't need to do reference checks, because two board members were personally vouching for Tom. If they have worked with Tom before, and they say Tom is the best, and the other board members like Tom, well, what am I worrying about?

I already have the reference checks done, right? Wrong! Dumb, dumb, and dumber! You should always do reference checks.

B. Backdoor reference checks.

It is a connected world, and everyone knows everyone. I could have easily done backdoor checks on Tom. You have to take in context what you are hearing but checking with mutual contacts about a candidate is essential.

Why are backdoor checks so important? You tend to get more candid answers than you do from the references the candidate suggests.

C. You should wait until the facts match your instincts.

You need to keep to your disciplines. I was under a lot of pressure to hire someone, and I let the pressure to hire make me move more quickly than I should have.

The Board really liking Tom didn't match my gut instinct that something was wrong. I should have kept digging, until the facts and my instincts matched up. I didn't, and it nearly cost us our funding.

I'm smarter than that. I suspect you are too. I should have been disciplined. When you're hiring, so should you.

Those voices in my head? They're still at it.

What Can You Learn From Successful Non-Technical CEOs?

"**D**on't try and be something that you're not." That was the advice I gave to myself, when I started my company.

Even though I have a BSEE and a few patents, I'd been on the "dark side," as Blossom calls the business side of a technology company, for years. I wasn't going to be the technical heart and soul of the company.

The challenges I had were similar to the unique challenges a completely non-technical CEO would have. You can trace all of the unique challenges back to the concept of "Don't try and be something that you're not."

I think there are three unique challenges that all non-technical CEOs face:

A. You need to hire a great VP Engineering or CTO.

"Who's your VP of Engineering going to be?" That was the question that Jack, a VC who was preparing to give us a term sheet, asked me.

The original founding VP Engineering, "John," quit almost a year before. I was running engineering on an interim basis, so I told Jack the truth. "I'm running engineering for now, until we find a replacement."

"That's what I thought you would tell me," Jack said. "However, there's too much risk for me to invest, until you find a full-time VP Engineering."

I didn't argue with Jack, because he was right. I was also pretty close to adding Jeroen to the team as our new VP Engineering. Two weeks later, I sent Jack an email letting him know we added Jeroen to the team. I included his resume.

Jack instantly responded. "Great. His resume is very impressive. Set up a meeting for me with him. I'll give you a term sheet, if the meeting goes well." The meeting between Jeroen and Jack went well, so we received a term sheet.

The reality is that you will not be perceived as being strong enough technically by investors.

Don't try and be something that you're not. Hire a great VP Engineering that can help you. This leads directly to point number two...

B. You need to recruit great technical talent.

You've brought on a great VP Engineering. Yes, your great VP Engineering is also going to co-lead the technical recruiting effort.

However, guess who the other technical recruiting

co-lead is? That's right, it's you.

In my case, about half of the founding engineering team came from my efforts, and the other half came from Jeroen's efforts. That doesn't mean that I didn't interview the engineers Jeroen recruited.

You're going to need to interview all the early engineering hires your company makes. The key is not to try to be something that you're not.

Mark my words. You will fail, if you try to prove how technically strong you are. Great engineers will instantly see you as a fraud.

Your first job is to evaluate potential engineers for their cultural fit in the company. Your second job is selling potential engineers on your vision for the company.

You don't need to be a technical wizard to do this. You do need to ask good questions, listen well and clearly articulate the company's vision.

Now that your great technical team is in place, you can't just ignore the technical side.

C. You need to stay involved in the technical side of the business.

You still need to stay involved, heavily involved in fact, in the technical side of the business. I know this sounds like the reverse of what I've been saying, but it's not. Let me explain.

Being heavily involved in the technical side of the business, doesn't mean that you're going to be trying to solve the technical issues your team will face. Being heavily involved in the technical side of the business does mean that you will be using your common sense to ask questions.

The best non-technical CEO I ever saw do this was the late Jack Gifford at Maxim Integrated Products. Gifford had a BSEE, but he had been on the marketing and sales side for years before he founded Maxim.

That didn't stop him from asking logical, probing questions of the technical team, when things went wrong. "Why didn't we ask that," was a constant theme you heard walking out of a meeting with Gifford.

You also want to stay heavily involved in the product and feature direction of your technical team. This again just requires your common sense.

Let me give you an example. To stay ahead in key product areas, we needed to develop a product that could operate from +2.7V and double the voltage for a key part of the device to greater than +5V.

There are well-known circuit techniques that use an inductor and a capacitor off chip to do this. However, our customers didn't want to use expensive inductors. They only wanted us to use cheap capacitors.

Chuck, a brilliant engineer, said it couldn't be done. I challenged Chuck and said, "Why not. It seems possible to me." Chuck was pissed. It was a Friday afternoon, and he stormed out of the meeting and, presumably, went home.

Monday morning, Chuck walked into my office and slammed a piece of paper on my desk. No, it wasn't his resignation. Instead, it was a new circuit technique that would allow us to do what we wanted to do.

I wasn't trying to be something that I wasn't. You can do the same thing. Just be logical and don't be afraid to ask the tough questions.

How Do You Run Your Company as Headcount Grows?

I remember there were six of us, after we closed our funding. There was myself, my four co-founders and our operations manager, Dave.

Two weeks later, Sid joined as our design engineering director. Within two months, we added three more design engineers, which brought us to ten employees.

We held company meetings every Friday afternoon in the large conference room next to my office. We had one row of cubicles (that we bought for $100) that everyone sat in. There was room for four more rows of cubes, before we ran out of space, which we would a couple of years down the road.

The environment at this early stage was intimate.

When you're in a small team environment, you get to know everyone very well. That's the beauty of a really early stage startup.

You should take advantage of this stage of your company's development to build strong bonds with you and your team.

You'll likely be in the process of recruiting and building the first product at the same time. There will be a lot of pressure (and there should be) to get the product out.

Don't lose focus on the importance of your company culture. Bringing in the so-called "brilliant jerk," can have a devastating effect on your long-term company culture.

It is very tempting to bring in the brilliant jerk, who will keep your project on schedule. Don't do it. The brilliant jerk will lay waste to your team in the process.

One of the things we did, at this early stage, was set up the meetings and processes for later.

At the beginning, we were mostly a bunch of engineers working on the various products we were developing. Everything was focused on getting these products out on schedule.

Thursday morning at 10 AM, we had our weekly engineering meeting. We went over each product in development, updated the schedule as needed and talked about how to help any engineer that might be in trouble.

Friday afternoon at 1:30 PM was my favorite meeting. It was the Crazy Idea meeting. What's a Crazy Idea meeting you ask? It's a meeting where anyone in the company can propose a new product idea.

The idea could just be one sentence, or it could be fully fleshed out. The only rule we had, was that the author of an idea would get feedback on what we liked or disliked about the idea.

The meeting was a great way for us to brainstorm new products. Sometimes, a one sentence idea would lead to a debate about how to make the idea better. A week or two later, the idea would turn into a full-fledged product that we would approve for development.

Over time, the meeting morphed to every other week. We mixed it up between new product ideas and engineers educating the other engineers on various technologies, engineering techniques and end market needs.

The early focus on company culture and processes will pay off, as your company grows.

I was really lucky because we had a really strong founding team. We already had a full executive staff, when we started.

The whole team of founders and our initial employees came from Maxim and Linear Technology. These two companies were considered the best of the best in the Analog IC world.

Fortunately, both companies were very entrepreneurial. Therefore, everyone was used to the speed of being at a startup. We also took the best practices, especially the best engineering practices we learned from Maxim and Linear, including:

A. A rigorous design review process.

Move fast and break things might work at Facebook, but it would destroy you when a tape out (that's the engineering file that gets sent to the fabrication facility to build your silicon) costs you more than $100,000.

Design reviews were tough. Engineers had to present their design to a peer review.

Jeroen, our VP Engineering, managed the process. Because we hired people that fit our culture (no brilliant jerks), the senior engineers heavily participated in the reviews.

The result was we had over 50% first silicon success, which was our plan.

B. A rigorous product introduction process.

After I left Maxim, I worked as a general manager of a competitor to Maxim. This company wasn't nearly as well run as Maxim.

Each division general manager was incentivized to meet their quarterly new product introduction goals. There's nothing wrong with that, except there was no oversight.

In other words, each general manager could release a product, even if it wasn't ready for production. There was often no collateral, so customers wouldn't know how to use the product.

It was a mistake that I didn't want to repeat at my company.

We, therefore, had a checklist of things required to release every product:

- Acceptable engineering yields
- Test programs ready
- Stock at all our distributors
- Samples ready
- Evaluation boards ready
- Collateral ready
- Advertisements ready

All this attention to detail helped us scale and announce multiple products each month.

The challenge as you grow, is not creating more needless rules.

Read the Netflix Culture Manifesto, if you haven't already. This slide (#43) is the real challenge you face, as your company grows:

> **Our model is to *increase* employee freedom as we grow,** rather than limit it, to continue to attract and nourish innovative people, so we have better chance of sustained success

NETFLIX

Most companies add more and more rules as they grow. That was certainly the case at the company I joined after leaving Maxim.

The CEO, "Bob," added rule after rule. He even had a rule about not eating lunch at your desk!

This is obviously not the environment you want at your company. You'll have to fight to achieve it, because every time something breaks, you'll be tempted to add another rule.

Don't do it. Learn from the Netflix model. Push the decision making down in your company and let your team learn from their mistakes.

ROUND 13: HOW SHOULD YOU THINK ABOUT SELLING YOUR BUSINESS?

Should You Sell Your Company or Take An Investment?

"**I**'m sorry Brett, but we're not going forward with the investment," "Robbie" said to me. The week before, Robbie and the other members of the investment syndicate had signed the term sheet. Now they were pulling out of the deal.

I spent the next hour on the phone convincing Robbie to stay in the deal. Fortunately for us, Robbie agreed to talk with his partners about staying in the deal.

What would happen to Robbie's fund, if they pulled out of the deal? Nothing.

Here's the thing: Your term sheet is a non-binding document.

You may have noticed that there was a statement in the term sheet that you signed saying something like, "This is a non-binding document." In other words, either party can walk away from the agreement before funding closes.

I called Gill, one of our existing investors, after I

got off the phone with Robbie. Gill's response was, "We're seeing this more and more that VCs are walking away from signed term sheets."

You need to do what's right for you.

I'm not saying you shouldn't take your commitment to the signed term sheet seriously. I am saying that you have to act in your company's best interest.

Let's say you have an offer to sell the company and you have a term sheet from a good investor. In this case, you need to evaluate the offer you are getting to sell the company. If the offer is a good offer that you want to accept, then you need to come to an agreement with the buyer to sell the company.

However, guess what that means?

If you decide to sell the company, you will sign some sort of memorandum of understanding or letter of intent with the buyer. In other words, you just signed another term sheet.

Selling a company is just like closing a funding round. You have to go through a diligence process. There's always an out for the buyer, if they decide to terminate the process.

There's no guarantee that the buyer of your company is actually going to buy the company.

Everything will be vetted during the diligence process. This includes your financials, contracts with vendors, contracts with customers and any loans that you have. All of it will be reviewed in detail. Any problem that the buyer finds, might a reason to terminate the deal.

You have to be intellectually honest about how real the offer is to buy your company.

For example, I'm working with someone right now that has an offer from a very large public company to buy his company. They've already agreed to the basic terms.

All that's left is for the CEO of the large public company to sign off on the deal. The deal was supposed to be signed by Tuesday. It's now Thursday and the deal hasn't been signed yet.

The reality is that there is risk, until the money is in the bank. The same is also true with VC funding. You are the only one who will have a sense of urgency, in either case, to close your funding or sell your company.

What Are the Five Signs It's Time To Sell Your Company?

A couple of years ago, I was advising a CEO. "Mark" had bootstrapped his company to profitability.

Mark's company began by providing consulting services. Mark's company then provided IP to its customers, along with consulting services.

The firm had grown to become a multi-million dollar revenue company. However, Mark had become increasingly worried lately.

Over lunch one day, Mark said to me, "Brett, I think we've tapped our technology as far as it can go. I think I should sell the company."

I agreed with Mark that it was time to sell the company. I started working with Mark on an acquisition strategy.

We developed a list of possible acquirers, and we figured out how we would begin working to get Mark's company acquired.

We were about a month into the process, when Mark called me and said, "Brett, I've changed my mind. I don't want to sell the company anymore."

I asked Mark what changed his mind. Mark said, "I just don't want to work for a big company again."

Did Mark make the right decision? Only time will tell. However, Mark's challenge is the one that all startup founders, and especially bootstrapped, startup founders face, if they are lucky:

When, if ever, do you sell your company?

I'm going to diverge for a bit about a story about thinking on your feet. You'll see how it fits in a bit.

I did a ton of public speaking as CEO. You probably have to as well, I imagine. Sometimes you're presenting to customers. Sometimes it is to your investors or board members. Other times you're being interviewed by the trade press. There are also times when you're presenting to your employees.

I once gave a talk to our employees, saying that all employees (including me) needed to go on minimum wage. It was a tough message to give them.

The day before I gave that talk, I spent four hours working with the executive staff on what type of questions I would get and how I should answer the questions.

Sometimes my initial answers were good. However, more often than not, my initial answers needed to be tweaked.

The preparation paid off.

I was prepared and ready to go by the next day. We had correctly anticipated many of the questions the employees would have.

There were still some questions that we didn't see coming. However, the preparation we did the day before, allowed me to quickly and confidently answer the questions the team had.

What does preparing yourself to answer questions, have to do with selling your company?

The key word is preparation.

You're dead, if you just expect someone to come along and make an offer to buy your company. You will not know what to do, even if someone does come along and make you an offer.

That's how you think on your feet. It's all about preparation.

It's important for you to have a plan of when you would sell your company.
Start by asking yourself the following questions:

A. How do you know what's right?

B. When is the right time to sell?

C. What price do I want for the company?

D. How do I know I'm getting a good deal?

E. Will the money make me happy?

F. What about my employees?

G. What's going to happen to me, if I sell?

H. What's going to happen to my family, if I sell?

Start taking steps now.

Don't worry. This doesn't mean you're selling your company. It just means you're being prudent.

Here are three easy steps you should take:

A. Research the market.

Look at recent transactions. What are other companies selling for in your market? You've got data now, if nothing else.

B. Establish relationships.

Why not get to know your competition? This doesn't mean you're selling the company. However, establishing CEO-to-CEO relationships or CEO to senior executive relationships can only help you.

C. Get a lawyer.

You will need legal representation, so get a lawyer that specializes in working with your type of company. Your lawyer will be critical to you, in any sale or merger.

One final step to prepare: Dealing with investment

bankers and brokers.

As my company grew in stature and size, I started getting phone calls from investment bankers. They wanted to meet with me.

It was way too early for us to sell, but I took the meetings. I would update them on the progress of the company.

In return, the bankers might pass along competitive or market data that was helpful to me. They might also make an introduction to someone helpful to the company. I even used the relationship with an investment banker to help with due diligence, when we were raising money.

Over time, relationships build.

You want a relationship in advance of when, and if, you make the decision to sell your company. You want to be working with someone you have a level of trust with.

Why should you work with an investment banker or broker?

It's actually pretty simple: You'll get maximum value for your company, by hiring an investment banker or broker.

Investment bankers and brokers have relationships with all the potential buyers. They can create a level of competition or perceived competition that gets you the best price.

When should you sell your company?

Selling your company is an extremely personal and emotional decision. You are literally selling a piece of yourself, when you sell your company.

That is why preparation is so important. Preparation will keep you focused on doing the right thing, and not the emotionally easy thing to do.

I'm not advocating that everyone should sell their company. You might be one of the lucky ones, where you can run your company for the rest of your career.

Maybe you'll be one of the extremely rare CEOs that oversee an IPO. Congratulations to you, if you are that fortunate.

However, even public companies merge or are acquired. It is more likely than not that your company will be sold someday.

How do you know it's time to sell your company?

Let's circle back to my friend Mark. Mark had taken his company as far as he could.

That's a good time to sell: When you can't see a way to grow the brand.   Mark, as I mentioned earlier, backed out at the last second. Only time will tell, if Mark made the right decision.

Here are four other good times to sell your company:

A. You're tired.

It's getting harder and harder to gather the strength to fight each day. This is a good time to sell.

B. The market price goes way up.

Bubbles where the market price increases irrationally, happen all the time in business. Think about the decision Mark Cuban made selling Broadcast.com to Yahoo! for $5.7 billion in 2000.

C. You can see the market for your products is changing, and maybe not in a good way.

This is the decision Mark has to make.

The good news is, you can usually see the market changes before the market does. A good example is Richard Branson selling Virgin Records in the 1990's, before the changes in the record industry.

D. You need the money or want the liquidity.

The Silicon Valley, where I live, is littered with stories of paper millionaires that got greedy and never made any money.

It's perfectly okay to make a business decision to take the money and sell your company.

When shouldn't you sell your company?

The anti of the list above is a pretty good place to start. If everything is going well and:

You're enjoying what you're doing, and...

The valuation for your company hasn't gone through the roof, and...

The market for your products isn't changing in a bad way, and...

You don't need the money or want the liquidity, then...

Keep doing what you're doing. However, stay the course, if all four of the above conditions are met. Otherwise, it might be time to consider selling your company.

Selling your company is one of the most emotional things you'll ever do in your life. Richard Branson said, "It's like selling your children." Selling your company is like selling your children, because a piece of you is forever gone.

However, the emotional pain of selling your company doesn't make selling your company the wrong decision. The careful preparation you take in advance of selling your company, can help you do the right thing when the time comes.

Why You Shouldn't Build
Your Startup to Be Acquired

There was a time in the late 1990's, when venture capitalists made a killing investing in semiconductor companies. The companies these VCs invested in were never meant to be companies built for the long term. Instead, they were meant to be flipped and sold quickly.

The flipping of companies in the late 1990's was a great strategy, until it wasn't anymore. The comms bubble burst in 2000. With the bursting of the comms bubble, went the ability to flip companies.

However, the bursting of the comms bubble didn't stop semiconductor entrepreneurs from believing that the right way to get funded was with the goal of being acquired. The bursting of the comms bubble also didn't stop VCs from continuing to pour money into semiconductor startups.

Let's be clear. You're not building a company, if your intent is to sell it.

Just like the semiconductor entrepreneurs of the late 1990's, you're not really building a company. You're maybe building a product. It may look somewhat like a company from the outside, but it's not really a company.

Real companies have a long-term strategy.

Real companies have a vision.

Your vision is just to be bought. What happens if, just like with the semiconductor entrepreneurs of the post bubble 2000's, you can't sell your company? Then what do you do?

You make too many compromises, when you start a company with the goal of quickly selling it.

You're screwed, if you can't sell your company quickly. That's the problem with the build to sell strategy.

A few years ago, a friend of mine, "Kevin," was convinced that he needed to sell his company. Kevin stopped investing in R&D, reduced his marketing spend and prepped the company for a sale.

After trying to sell the company for nine months, Kevin realized that the price he was going to get for his company wasn't what he thought he would get. Kevin now had to restart everything.

You want to build your company, as if it's never going to get sold.

Kevin's story is an example of what can happen to you, when stop focusing on the long- term. He lost at least 12 months of momentum, maybe more, by focusing on a sale.

I've also seen the same thing happen with other entrepreneurs. You want to build your company for the long term.

A few interesting things started happening with us, as we started gaining more and more market traction:

A. We started getting requests from market analysts to talk with us

B. Investment banks wanted to meet with us

C. Public companies in our space wanted to meet with us

I took every meeting. I didn't want to sell the company, but I thought it was good to meet people and start building contacts.

Interestingly enough, the contacts paid off, but not in the way you might think. Some of our potential investors wanted to speak with an analyst, so I introduced the investors to Tore. One of the investment banks we met with introduced us to a potential strategic (public company) investor. Finally, one of the public companies we met with became an investor in our next round.

20 Hidden Benefits
From Losing Your Job or
Selling Your Company

It was Sunday night at 11 PM, when I heard the phone ring. The second I heard the phone ring, I knew my dad was dead.

My mom told me the paramedics were at the house, but dad was gone. "I need you here tomorrow," she said.

Blossom and I hurriedly arranged to fly down to Los Angeles on the first flight Monday morning. We arranged for our two-year-old daughter, Avery, to stay with my in-laws.

My mom was waiting at the front door of the house, when we got to her house. I was barely holding myself together, but I just started crying when I saw my mom.

There was also laughter. That night, my brother and I watched the Chicago Bears make an improbable rally against the Arizona Cardinals on Monday Night Football. Dad grew up in Chicago, and he was a huge Chicago Bears fan. We were too. We laughed that dad had blown Arizona's last-second field goal attempt wide of the goal posts.

I cried several times over the next couple days, as we made the various arrangements that we all need to make when someone close to us dies. It was really tough.

Losing my dad paled in comparison to selling my company.

I know it sounds shocking, but it's true. Losing my dad paled in comparison to selling my company.

You know your parents are going to eventually die. It's heartbreaking, but natural. Nothing in my life has knocked me on my butt, like the aftermath of selling my company.

Probably the closest thing to the aftermath of selling a company, is being fired. I've been fired twice and being fired is really tough.

Maybe it is because we wanted to go forward and one of our investors forced us to sell.

Maybe it is because the surviving business has done really well since it was sold, and I know it would be REALLY fun to be running the company at this stage.

I don't know.

You are the hub of everything, when you are CEO of a company. Running a company is a real high. Even the bad days are good, and, believe me, there were many bad days.

You go from being the hub of everything to, well, not being the hub of everything.

The reality is that a piece of you is removed from your soul, when your company is sold.

You can never get that piece of your soul back.

You can learn about yourself when you are fired, or you quit your job, or you are forced to sell your company like I had to do. Here are 20 positive things you can gain:

A. You are more resilient than you realize.

You have just been punched in the mouth, but you realize you survived.

B. You can reconnect with your family.

I was so focused on building my company, that it occupied just about every waking moment. It is the price of success, but it comes at the expense of your family. I've gotten to spend a lot more quality time with my family this past year.

C. You can go on walks with your wife.

Blossom and I now walk together two or three times a week. It is just the two of us. There is more time to reconnect and spend quality time together.

D. You can learn about another industry.

In my case, it is the online world. I've spent my

whole career on the hardware side of things.

Part of the last year I learned how the online world ticks. It turns out that it's not much different than hardware.

E. You can write about your experiences.

Writing is great for the soul. You don't have to publish your thoughts like I do. However, writing in a journal is very therapeutic.

F. You can read more books.

You can also take advantage of audible.com. Go for a run, listen to a book and learn at the same time. Fantastic!

G. You can educate yourself through the world of podcasts and YouTube.

Watch a Ted talk and learn or listen to a podcast, while on the go.

H. You can talk to your brother more often.

I do. Russell and I were always close, and now we are closer.

I. You can take your daughter to school every day.

I used to take Avery to school once a week or so. More often than not, I now get to take Avery to school. I get to hear her practice singing on the way to school. She's got a really good voice!

J. You can lose 25 pounds.

I did. I went on the LeBron James diet. What is the LeBron James diet you ask? Meat, fish, fruit, veggies and nuts. I had crazy dreams at the beginning about the chocolate cake I was missing, but it was worth it.

K. You can still accomplish amazing things.

Yes, things have changed, but anything is possible. In my case, my friend Cathal and I convinced an investor to invest $70 million, based on an idea we had over coffee at Peet's.

L. You can start another business.

I am. I don't know the number of businesses that get started because someone's job situation changed, but I'll bet it is a very large number.

M. You realize that success is not measured by what others think.

Success is measured by what you think. Eventually, your self-worth comes back. You realize that you are a success, and you are good.

N. You can learn about meditation and mindfulness.

All it takes is 15 to 20 minutes a day. Your mind slows down, and you feel fantastic. Read, Zen Mind, Beginner's Mind, if you are interested.

O. You realize that you need to continually chal-

lenge myself.

I need to push myself to be happy. I am unhappy, when I am not challenged.

P. You can mentor a lot of people.

I've gotten to work with many talented people in fields other than mine during the past year. You realize that your skills are not limited just to your narrow field of expertise.

Q. You can give a talk to your friend's entrepreneurship class.

My good friend Dave asked me to speak to his entrepreneurship class at the University of San Francisco. It was very cool. It felt great giving back.

R. You can learn how to sleep without Ambien.

Yes, the "other" blue pill. I was so stressed because of the fights we were having with one of our investors, that Ambien was the only way I could get four hours of sleep.

S. You can become a Fitbit fanatic.

Our friends Rob and Sue gave us Fitbits for the holidays. The only problem is Blossom is ALWAYS is ahead of me in step count. Pisses me off :-).

T. You can grow an inch.

I took my annual physical last week. The first thing the nurse did was measure my height. "5'11" she said. You've grown an inch." Cool! Now I just need to grow one more inch and I'm back to where I was when I was 30.

I don't know how things will turn out.

None of us do.

I do know this:

I have more good days than bad days.

I am happy.

I am the luckiest man in the world.

Wrigley Field, Chicago. August 2007.

My Mom, Blossom, Avery, and I were in left field, near the warning track, about to scatter my dad's ashes in the outfield. My Mom engineered this, through her friend's connections.

All I could think was, "This is really cool!"

My other thought was, "Did my dad just enter purgatory? He's going to see a lot of misery."

I had never been on the field at Wrigley before.

My childhood flashes back in an instant: There we are. My dad, grandfather, brother and me taking the "L" to see the Cubs play at Wrigley.

"Let's play two!" I said to myself.

ABOUT THE AUTHOR

Brett J. Fox

Do You Want To Grow Your Business? Maybe I Can Help.

I love startups! I mean, I absolutely love startups!
I love the struggle. I love the sense you're building something big. I love the thrill of getting a product to market and watching revenue grow.

But, it's not easy, is it? Sometimes it feels like you are climbing Mount Everest alone.
I know that feeling all too well...

I've been exactly where you've been.

I know how difficult raising money truly is (63 Venture Capital Firms turned us down before the 64th funded my company). I know how tough it is to get traction in the marketplace. You get there by grinding every day.

I know how tough it is to really build a world-class company. I know what it's like to epically fail, and I know what it's like to win big.

My Promise to You:

I will not pull any punches, and I will not hold back any information. You'll get everything I know.

You can learn from all my experiences:

- How to avoid my failures
- How to take a punch and keep moving forward
- How to replicate (and exceed) my successes

I am here to help you win!

Join my mailing list and get your free 10 point Startup CEO Checklist. Just go to www.brettj-fox.com/bookchecklist, and you'll learn how I built several businesses from $0 to >$100M, raised over $100M in venture capital and private equity funding, built world-class teams, developed products that were 10X to 100X better than the competition, dealt with crazy investors, survived The Great Recession and lived to talk about it.

I look forward to helping you achieve success!

Brett Fox

Did you enjoy Learn How To Take A Punch? You can make a big difference.

Reviews are the most powerful way for me to grow the awareness of my writing. If you enjoyed Learn How To Take A Punch, then I'd really appreciate it if you took a few minutes to share your thoughts.

Thanks!

Brett